THE
HUDSON RIVER
VALLEY

THE
HUDSON RIVER
VALLEY
A History and Guide

Tim Mulligan

Illustrations by Stan Skardinski

Random House • New York

A portion of this work was first published in *Travel & Leisure*, in
different form.

Library of Congress Cataloging in Publication Data
Mulligan, Tim, 1938–
The Hudson River valley.
Includes index.
1. Hudson River Valley (N.Y. and N.J.)—History.
2. Hudson River Valley (N.Y. and N.J.)—Description and
travel—Guide-books. 3. Historic sites—Hudson River
Valley (N.Y. and N.J.)—Guide-books. I. Title.
F127.H8M88 1985   974.7'3   84-18227
ISBN 0-394-73099-2 (pbk.)

Manufactured in the United States of America
456789

Design by Bernard Klein

*To Celia Rhoads Mulligan,
whose love, patience and understanding
have smoothed many a rocky road*

SPECIAL ACKNOWLEDGMENT

Special thanks are due to John O'Keefe, whose contributions have been so great that he became the co-developer of this project. From its inception his sage advice, participation in various Hudson River forays and almost uncanny sense of and feel for the river have had a profound influence on the shape of the book. Without his influence, whatever is of value in these pages would be significantly lessened.

AUTHOR'S NOTE

The distance covered by this book, from New York City to Saratoga, is one that can be done in a five-hour drive. It is relatively easy, therefore, to go from any place mentioned in the Upper Hudson section to, say, one listed in the Lower Hudson. I suggest that, if you can, you consider taking the train. The ride from New York to Albany offers unparalleled views of the river, making it one of the country's great train trips, because most of the track runs along the east bank.

I do not list motels—see one, you've seen them all—but they are there, in run-of-the-mill abundance, if you cannot get a reservation at one of the inns, bed & breakfasts or hotels mentioned in this book. In addition, you can obtain a complete listing of bed & breakfast lodgings in the valley by writing to: Bed & Breakfast USA, Ltd., P.O. Box 606, Croton-on-Hudson, NY 10520. Include $1 for the brochure and a stamped, self-addressed envelope.

Two other things. First, I have decided to follow the Hudson from Saratoga south to New York City for the purely arbitrary reasons that to me it feels right going with the flow of the river rather than against it, and that the logical culmination for the book is in New York City, where the Hudson disappears under the great harbor. Second point: If death and taxes are inevitable, so are rising prices. All figures given were accurate as the book went to press, but there could—and probably will—be upward variations. By the same token, hours may also vary. If you are operating on a tight schedule, it would be wise to call in advance.

Finally, this is a personal book that reflects my tastes and opinions. It is not a compendium of everything in the valley; moreover, as you will see, I do not pretend to like every place I describe—and I will tell you why. I have written this book as I would talk to a friend, giving information that I hope will be enjoyed. I hope, too, if you find something you would like to pass along, that you will not hesitate to write me.

ACKNOWLEDGMENTS

An extraordinary number of people have extended themselves to help, counsel and guide me in the creation of this book. Several of these deserve a formal acknowledgment.

I would like to thank Jerry Aiello, a longtime devotee of the River, who was always ready for yet one more visit on the Hudson and whose gentle perceptions added a great deal to my own observations.

Frank and Fernanda Gilligan gave me their home in the Valley several times to serve as a "base of operations" and were hospitality itself, as was Lillian Phipps, who made one visit to Saratoga among my most memorable stays in the Valley.

Fred Johnston, who appears in these pages, was both among the first to open my eyes to the depth and splendor of the Valley and also has been a loyal supporter of my efforts to capture something of the feel of the Hudson River Valley.

Pamela Fiori, editor of *Travel & Leisure,* gave me the opportunity to write extensively on the Hudson and has long been not only one of my favorite people but also is a superb and wise editor.

My thanks, too, to Rita Martin, a warm and caring lady, who kept me alive on glorious foods while I was trying to meet my deadlines, and to Karen Emmons who cheerfully translated an extremely confusing manuscript.

And, finally, heartfelt thanks to my editor, Cheryl Merser, patient, wise and trusting, who believed in this book from the first time we discussed it. She gave me all the help and support any writer could ask for. She has become my friend as well as my editor. Toward completion of the project, Melanie Fleishman added her help and she, too, did everything in her power to be supportive.

To all the others who were in one way or another involved in this venture, thank you. Needless to say, the good things come from all of them; the bad are mine alone.

CONTENTS

The Lower Hudson: From Putnam County to New York City

INTRODUCTION

I HAVE lived near the Hudson many, many years, and throughout that time I have watched the life on this great river—
freighters and tugs, the last of the great ocean liners, fireworks
on the Fourth of July, sunsets that could have been painted by
Turner or Monet or Church, great cakes of ice clustering around
the piers in winter, sailboats and yachts in summer.

Familiarity has made the Hudson central to my life. It is the
one timeless and unchanging part of New York City, the anchor
that, to borrow from Gertrude Stein, lets you know there *is* a
"there" there. It is comforting to know that there still are places
from which the Hudson looks exactly the same as it did to the
first settlers: from the Cloisters, for example. And the Palisades,
those wonderful walls of the Hudson, remain relatively unspoiled, the most beautiful natural feature left near the city.
But this is only the mouth of a river whose beauty is so great
that the first cohesive group of American artists, the Hudson
River School, formed to paint it and its surroundings in every
mood and season.

The Hudson is an ancient river whose beginnings go back
seventy-five million years. About sixty-five million years ago, as
the land rose, the river began cutting its valley between the
Catskill and Taconic mountains, down to the splendid Hudson
Highlands, and flowed first west, then east to empty into the
Atlantic Ocean. About ten million years ago, theory has it, a
smaller river moved northward and there, in the Highlands,
joined the Hudson, which abandoned its old course and now
flows south to the sea. More recently, during the Ice Age, the sea
level was lower than it is today, and the Continental Shelf was
exposed; the Hudson then flowed through this plain for 120
miles until it reached the sea. Today you may think the river
ends in the harbor, but it really is flowing onward, to the end
of the shelf, where it finally disappears into the Hudson Canyon
and the vastness of the Atlantic.

Because the Hudson's channel is below sea level from,
roughly, Troy on, ocean tides run up to Troy, making the river
an estuary. According to Robert H. Boyle, author of the brilliant

THE HUDSON RIVER VALLEY

book *The Hudson River: A Natural and Unnatural History,*
"More properly, the Hudson is a drowned river; after the last
glacier melted, rising seawater moved in and flooded the old
course of the river. Because of this, the lower Hudson is unusually deep and is suitable for navigation by ocean-going vessels
up to Albany."

As great rivers go, the Hudson is relatively small, only 315
miles long from its source to the ocean—by comparison, the
Mississippi is 2,348 miles long, the Seine 482 miles and the
Rhine 820 miles—and what most people see is simply that part
from Albany south, a distance of only 150 miles. But what extraordinary beauty it encompasses along this length. And what
an extraordinary amount of life it supports. Millions of fish live
here, both marine and freshwater species, making it, according
to Mr. Boyle, "the greatest single wildlife resource in New York
State."

It was only in 1872 that the true source of the Hudson was
located when Verplanck Colvin, an official surveyor for the
state of New York, discovered a tiny pond on the slopes of
Mount Marcy in the Adirondacks and knew that there was the
beginning of the river. In his report to the state legislature
Colvin wrote, "Far above the chilly waters of Lake Avalanche,
at an elevation of 4,293 feet, is Summit Water, a minute, un-
pretending tear of the clouds, as it were—a lovely pool shivering
in the breezes of the mountains, and sending its limpid surplus
through Feldspar Brook and to the Opalescent River, the wellspring of the Hudson." So moved were the legislators by Colvin's eloquence that they changed the name of Summit Water
to Lake Tear of the Clouds.

From there, for 161 miles until the river joins the Mohawk,
it flows southeast, mainly through unspoiled wilderness. Oddly
enough, this, one of the world's most famous rivers, is almost
unknown for a good part of its length, and yet in this seldom-
visited stretch is found some of its greatest drama—for instance, where the river rushes for a mile, churning and violent,
through the Hudson Gorge, a series of great cliffs that rise, in
some places, to eminences of more than 800 feet. Then, once out
of the Adirondacks, it grows placid, a gentle river flowing
through pretty fields on its way to Albany.

From Albany the river passes through scenery so diverse and

appealing that many people find it the most beautiful river valley in the world. "Perpetually interesting," Henry James said of the Hudson, and so it is, with the stunning Catskill Mountains, the brooding intensity of the Hudson Highlands, the greatest city in the world at its mouth and an extraordinary bounty of things to see and do that can keep you going back for years to revel in them.

The river was first discovered in 1524 by Giovanni da Verrazano, who was exploring the coast of North America for Francis I, king of France. But it was not until 1609, when Henry Hudson, on a voyage sponsored by the Dutch and mistakenly thinking the river might lead to the Orient, sailed as far north as Albany, that it truly entered our history. Since then, millions upon millions of immigrants have arrived in America on the Hudson's waters, and almost every ethnic group has left its distinguishing mark on the river valley. In the eighteenth century, control of the river, the colonists' most important "highway," meant control of the country, and during the American Revolution one third of the battles were fought along its shores. Indeed, arguably the most important conflict of the war took place here, the Battle of Saratoga, which decided once and for all that the British would not gain control of the vital waterway.

Then, in the nineteenth century, with the opening of the Erie Canal, the development of the West could move ahead in earnest, helping to make New York a world metropolis and the economic center of the nation. It was the Hudson that provided the foundation for the Empire State.

It was in the nineteenth century, too, that the river experienced its most brilliant development. The steamboat got its start when Robert Fulton first sailed the *Clermont*—"a boat driven by a teakettle," some said—from New York to Albany in thirty-two hours. Great estates appeared, a long line of them along both banks of the river, that made the Hudson into America's own Loire Valley. Cities arose, grew and prospered. Trade flourished. And the painters sent out their impressions of the valley, first to the nation, then to the world, while thousands came to see and share the magnificence.

Today the valley is tinged with an aura of romance and wrapped in that famous, unique light still so much admired by artists and travelers alike. Like America, the Hudson River Valley has matured, even grown old—many canals are graceful ruins, the towns are in the throes of restoration, the estates have mostly become public institutions of one sort or another, the great families have either died out or retreated behind their walls as their wealth, like the early prosperity of the valley, has declined. But also like America, it has a new vitality stirring. IBM, a company that represents the future, is here, and with its presence and its thousands of employees have come prosperity and growth, making of this region an eastern version of Silicon Valley. And with prosperity and time and maturity has come a new awareness of the river and what it means to all of us.

THE
UPPER HUDSON
From Saratoga County
to Dutchess County

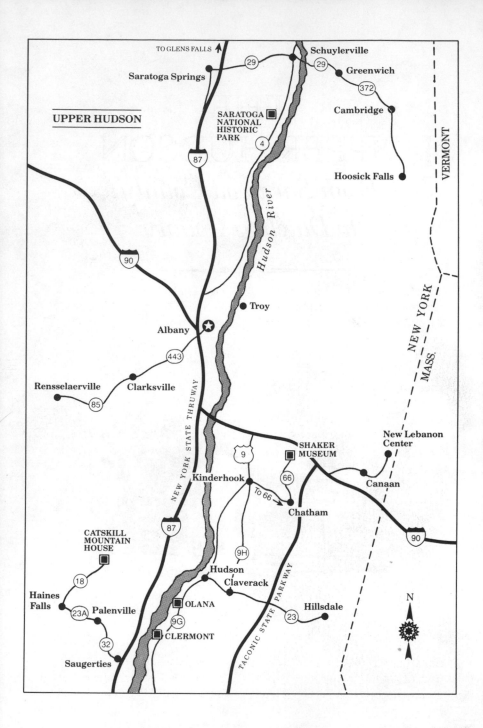

UPPER HUDSON

TO GLENS FALLS

Saratoga Springs

29

Schuylerville

29

Greenwich

372

Cambridge

SARATOGA
NATIONAL
HISTORIC
PARK

4

Hoosick Falls

87

VERMONT

Hudson River

90

Troy

Albany

443

NEW YORK

MASS.

Rensselaerville

Clarksville

85

NEW YORK STATE THRUWAY

New Lebanon
Center

SHAKER
MUSEUM

9

66

Canaan

Kinderhook

To 66

Chatham

87

90

CATSKILL
MOUNTAIN
HOUSE

9H

Hudson

Claverack

Haines
Falls

18

23A

Palenville

OLANA

TACONIC STATE PARKWAY

Hillsdale

23

9G

32

CLERMONT

Saugerties

N

THE Upper Hudson imparts a series of vibrantly colored and diverse impressions: jockeys in their brilliant shining silks entering the handsomest of racing courses at Saratoga; blues and greens and browns and russets spreading out for miles to the horizon, defining one of the more spectacular views in the nation; the cold formality of the Albany Mall, looking surreal in its essentially rural environs; gray-white cloud shadows, scudding like ghosts of soldiers above the battlefield of Saratoga; a museum dedicated to the Shakers—this area was their original home—set deep in the countryside within barn-red buildings and filled with exquisite creations echoing a simpler, more direct past. And through it all the Hudson, narrow and placid near Saratoga, vast and filled with traffic at Albany, blue and tranquil and looking rather gentrified at the old estate of Clermont at the southern tip of Columbia County.

The whole area builds like a pointillist painting. Each new experience or sight or building or museum adds another dot to the canvas and finally, once you've seen and felt it all and stand back, there it is, revealed in all its glory: a composition as lovely and complex as you could imagine, the Hudson at its heart, giving it, in many instances, its very reason for being.

The reader might think that, precisely because the Upper Hudson is so diverse, the distances must be great, too. Not so. You can easily drive from Saratoga Springs, the furthest point north, to Clermont in about two hours.

SARATOGA COUNTY

Saratoga Springs

Saratoga Springs, a town of slightly over 20,000 people, is the quintessential American resort. It always has been. By that, I mean that everyone—with money, without money, socially on

A door is a door is a door—except when an imaginative late Victorian decided he wanted it to make a Statement.

top or at the very bottom, racing tout or culture buff—did and does come here. They eat in the same restaurants, stay at the same hotels, ignore each other or mix as the mood moves them. It works beautifully. In fact, it's one reason the Springs is so alluring.

Today, more than ever before, it offers something for every taste: ballet, concerts, the baths, all kinds of sports, theater— and, of course, the world-famous track. I love to come here; it has a certain raffish charm quite unlike any other place.

HISTORY

The mineral springs were what originally made the village famous, but although the Indians had known about them for years, it was not until 1771 that the first white man of importance arrived. He was Sir William Johnson, the British general superintendent of Indian Affairs, who was suffering from a wound in his leg that refused to heal. The Iroquois, who were fond of him, bundled Johnson off to what would become known as High Rock Spring, and he later wrote of his "cure."

Nothing much happened after that until the end of the Revolutionary War—people had been too busy fighting to think about "taking the waters"—when Philip Schuyler, member of one of the most prominent families in the area, who had a country estate in what today is Schuylerville but then was the original town of Saratoga, cut a trail through to the spring in 1783 and brought to it such luminaries as Washington (he considered buying property there), Alexander Hamilton (he married Schuyler's daughter Betsy) and New York state governor George Clinton. Other prominent men of the time soon followed. (See page 38)

Then, in 1789, Gideon Putnam arrived and saw right away that he was sitting on a gold mine. He bought land near the recently discovered Congress Spring (named that because it was discovered by a member of Congress) and built the Springs' first hotel in 1802. Almost from its start it proved a success, so in 1805 Putnam purchased an additional 130 acres and laid out a village, donating land for a church, school and graveyard. Later would come the elm trees that were to be a distinguishing feature of Saratoga throughout the nineteenth century along Broadway, the avenue which Putnam had designed to run by his hotel.

The next big break for Saratoga came in 1826 when Dr. John Clarke, operator of the first soda fountain in New York City, began bottling and shipping water from the springs. By 1830, over 1,000 bottles a day were going out into the world. Saratoga was well on its way to becoming a household word, and the number of visitors began to increase proportionally. (By the end of the 1830's, 12,000 guests were arriving annually.) Dr. Clarke was also responsible for laying the foundations of one of the most pleasant spots in Saratoga, Congress Park. That was the plus side. On the minus end, according to some viewpoints (but not Saratoga's), the 1830's brought the introduction of heavy gambling, and in 1842 a man named Ben Scribner opened the first formal gambling parlor, starting a tradition that would last until the 1950's and for which Saratoga became as well known then as Las Vegas is today.

Two other events around this time helped immensely in the development of Saratoga: the use of steamboats on the Hudson and the introduction of the railroad. Together they changed the trip to the Springs from one that definitely *required* a cure at its end to a pleasant and relatively relaxing journey. By the 1850's, then, Saratoga was it; no other resort could touch its popularity. It had even caused the invention of the Saratoga trunk, a cavernous object large enough to hold a month's clothing.

In those days, too, a Saratogan made a major contribution to American cuisine. It was fashionable to repair to nearby Lake Saratoga in the late afternoon to dine, and the most famous of the establishments there was called Moon's Lake House, reasonably enough. The chef was a man with a ferocious temper, George Crum, son of a mulatto jockey and an Indian. He considered himself a superb cook—which he apparently was—and went into a rage if anyone ever dared complain about one of his delectable dishes. On a hectic night in 1853, a man sent back his French fried potatoes demanding they be cut thinner and fried crisper. George was not pleased. He proceeded to slice some potatoes paper thin, wrapped them in a napkin, and then covered them with chunks of ice. After letting his customer cool his heels for half an hour, George threw the equally cool potatoes into boiling oil. Once they were fried to a crisp, he sent them out to the table. A gesture of pure contempt that backfired—for lo and behold, the customer loved them! George had just invented the potato chip, which for many years afterward was known as the Saratoga chip.

The greatest and most flamboyant period of the Springs began with the end of the Civil War and continued until the close of the century, when it seemed that everywhere throughout the nation the opportunities to make vast amounts of money were endless, and those who did usually could think of no better place to spend it than here. They came in droves, and many of their descendants are still returning today.

This was the period of the great hotels, two of which—the Grand Union and the United States—are still talked about today. The Grand Union was a five-story behemoth that covered seven acres. Its 450-foot-long façade faced Broadway while at each end was a wing that extended back for a whole quarter of

The Adelphi Hotel, one of the last remnants of the great nineteenth-century hotels on Saratoga's Broadway whose primary ornaments were their great columned piazzas and fantasy-laden Victorian decorations.

a mile. The wings enclosed gardens, shaded by those famous Saratoga elms, and an opera house. There were 824 guest rooms, a main dining room that could serve a thousand at a clip (an additional room could take an overflow of up to four hundred diners), and a mile of piazzas filled with hundreds of wicker armchairs.

The United States Hotel wasn't much smaller, but its 50-foot pillars were distinguished by capitals of a singularly ugly Victorian design, some carver's nightmarish vision of jungle foliage.

This hotel had "cottages" with as many as seven bedrooms for its better-heeled clientele, but its overall length was only a quarter of a mile. Both the United States and the Grand Union devised a myriad of diverse activities for their guests, including lawn games and concerts every morning, afternoon and evening. (Victor Herbert, among others, conducted here.) It was grand, all right, but it's all gone, like Ozymandias' kingdom in Shelley's poem. ("Look on my works, ye Mighty, and despair! Nothing besides remains . . .") The United States was razed in 1946, the Grand Union in 1952. To add insult to injury, where the Grand Union once stood is now the site of an indescribably boring shopping center.

This was also the era of the great show-offs, some of whom took flamboyance to heights—or depths—rarely rivaled since. Probably the most outrageous in creative vulgarity was Diamond Jim Brady, who made $12 million by the time he was forty selling railroad equipment and whose close companion—they probably were never lovers—was the beauteous, amply-endowed Lillian Russell. The stories about Brady are legion. Item: Diamond Jim had thirty sets of jewels, one for (well, almost) each day of the month, that flashed out from everywhere on his person; even his underclothes sported jeweled buttons. In the most fabulous set—all to be worn at the same time, naturally—were more than 2,500 diamonds. Item: One year Brady arrived at the Springs in a silver-plated railroad car with 27 Japanese houseboys. Item: Enormous in girth as well as fortune, Diamond Jim was the possessor, it was said, of a stomach six times the normal size. (I imagine this is why contemporaries figured he wasn't doing much with Miss Lillian.) Brady never drank liquor or wine, but could easily down four gallons of freshly squeezed orange juice during a meal. To very special friends Diamond Jim often proved as generous as Maecenas. Consider the bicycle he gave Lillian: it was gold-plated, the handlebars studded with diamonds and emeralds that formed her initials. It must be said, the actress and the financier fitted in very well with the general Saratoga tone.

What to See and Do

Racing The racecourse at Saratoga, the oldest in the country, is the Queen Dowager of American tracks. During August, the racing season here, it turns the Springs into the capital of the race world and sets off a whirl of social activities that few other resorts can match.

The course was founded in 1863, when a track was built for thoroughbreds. Almost from the beginning three millionaire turf experts—stockbroker William R. Travers; John Hunter, a famous sportsman of the day; and Leonard Jerome, Winston Churchill's grandfather—were involved. The first season, a four-day, eight-race meeting, was a success, but the partners felt the track was too narrow and the grandstand too small, so they bought 125 acres across the road, landscaped them lavishly, erected a handsome grandstand—and, a year later, they were off and running. (The old course is still in use though, as a training track, and is now known as Horse Haven.) In that year, too, 1864, the Travers Stakes, the oldest and certainly one of the most prestigious racing events in America, was first run.

The track and all the surrounding buildings leave you with a vivid series of impressions: Petunias and flaming red geraniums in boxes everywhere . . . The elaborately carved horsehead decorations . . . The red-coated outriders escorting the horses and jockeys to the starting gate each day just before the 2:00 P.M. post time . . . The canoe in the lake in the infield, painted each year with the colors of the stable whose entry has captured the Travers Stakes . . . The elegant grandstand with its peaks and gables giving it a particularly jaunty air . . . The stables flying famous racing colors from all over the country . . . The thrill of watching the horses go through their early morning workouts while you enjoy breakfast at the track on red-and-white tablecloths, a color combination that seems to especially epitomize this track. (This breakfast ritual at the track anyone can share and no one should miss.) By post time the excitement is palpable. There is a sense of ceremony here, a long tradition that separates this course from all others. You don't even have to like racing to enjoy it. It is indeed the Dowager Queen.

The National Museum of Racing   This museum, located on Union Avenue right across from the track, is unique in the nation. It was formed in the early 1950's to collect, preserve and exhibit "all books, documents, printed matter and written material, statuary, memorials and any and all kinds of articles associated with the origin, history and development of horse racing and the breeding of thoroughbred horses." They're well along in their goal; there is, for example, the auctioneer's gavel that closed the sale of Man o' War, the most famous horse of this century, for $5,000 (he went on to win almost $250,000); an entire gallery devoted to the noted nineteenth-century equine artist Edward Troye; a cane given to a jockey by King Edward VII; a Charles Willson Peale portrait of George Washington, who liked to officiate at race meets; and hundreds of other paintings and portraits. There even are examples of the furniture that once graced the Grand Union and United States hotels, as well as an excellent reference library.

But my favorite exhibit is the more than 200 gloriously colorful racing silks belonging to every famous racing name in this country and including those of Queen Elizabeth II as well. (Racing colors originated in Newmarket, England, when it was agreed in 1762 that owners should choose specific colors to be worn by their jockeys and that these colors would then be reserved for their exclusive use. In this country, most colors are registered with the Jockey Club.) Open: April–December, Monday–Friday 9:30–5; May–December, also open Saturday 12–5; mid-June to mid-September, also open Sunday 12–5; January–March, Monday–Friday 10–4; August racing meet, 9:30–7 daily. Closed January 1, Thanksgiving and Christmas day. Admission: Free. Phone: 518-584-0400.

The Casino and Congress Park   In 1861, John Morrissey, ex-boxer and "enforcer" for Tammany Hall, the notoriously corrupt Democratic machine that ran New York City, opened a gambling casino in Saratoga on what is now Woodlawn Avenue. Born in Troy, New York, Morrissey made his first real money—$5,000—in a boxing match in California during the Gold Rush. Once back in New York, he rejoined the Tammany organization and served it so well that he was rewarded with his own gambling parlor. It proved a success, and soon John was the

A section of the Saratoga Casino, once the most elegant and fabulous gambling establishment in the nation and now a fading memory set in a pretty park.

leading gambler of New York City. But it was to Saratoga that he turned his full attention and talents; he was shrewd enough to recognize that here was the greatest potential moneymaker of his career. He was right.

In 1863 Morrissey helped to start thoroughbred racing; by that time he was a well-established figure on the Saratoga scene. With the end of the Civil War and the influx of new rich, though, Morrissey saw an even bigger opportunity and bought land adjoining Dr. John Clarke's Congress Spring estate. He then proceeded to build a Club House and landscape the grounds, creating the most impressive gambling establishment in the country. It's still there and is known now as the Casino.

The Club House opened in 1870 and immediately was the rage. It also included an elegant dining room for women, doubtless another reason why the Club House soon became the major center of Saratoga's social life. (To keep the natives from getting restless, Morrissey contributed heavily to local charities and would not allow them to gamble in his establishment—no chance of sour grapes if they couldn't lose their shirts.)

But Morrissey's days of wine and roses and cascading piles of gold were doomed. He made the mistake of taking thoroughly poor financial advice from Commodore Vanderbilt and quickly lost one million dollars. Added to which, his health was failing. In 1878, at the age of forty-seven, John Morrissey died.

The Club House then passed on to Albert Spencer and Charles Reed for several uneventful years until, in 1894, Richard A. Canfield, "Prince of Gamblers," bought and completely renovated the building, changing its name to the Casino. By 1900 Canfield was the most famous—and richest—gambler in the nation. Like Morrissey, Canfield had a colorful background. A man of little formal education, he was once thrown in prison for six months for illegal gambling. To while away the hours, he began to read and educate himself. This—and collecting works of art—became Canfield's passion and would remain so for the rest of his life. (James McNeill Whistler and Canfield later became friends, and the artist painted his portrait, slyly calling it "His Reverence.")

In 1902, Canfield bought the land adjoining the Casino and landscaped it into an Italian garden, which is now part of Congress Park. At the same time he also added the stunning restaurant, still the most beautiful room in the Casino building, with its barrel-vaulted ceiling set with octagonal windows. Unfortunately, though, the glory days for gamblers were coming to an end as reform sentiment swept across the country. The Casino did not open for the 1904 season, much to everyone's shock and chagrin, and, even worse, Canfield put it up for sale in 1907. No buyers were interested, and in 1911, the village trustees purchased it for $150,000, combining it with the adjacent section of Congress Park, which they had already acquired. Canfield himself died in 1914 in New York City after a fall down a subway stair.

Today the Casino is a pleasant museum displaying the history of Saratoga Springs, including a particularly handsome Victorian parlor with an excellent sampling of furniture by John Henry Belter, the German-born cabinetmaker whose New York City shop turned out some of the finest examples of Victorian furnishings produced in this country. In addition there are other historical rooms, as well as changing art exhibits and a museum gift shop.

Open daily: Memorial Day weekend, June, September and October, Monday–Saturday 10–4, Sunday 1–4; July and August, daily 9:30–4:30; November 2–Memorial Day weekend, Wednesday–Sunday 1–4. Admission: $1; senior citizens and students, 50¢. Phone: 518-584-6920.

Saratoga Performing Arts Center (SPAC) In the early 1960's, a group of Saratogans suggested to then-Governor Nelson Rockefeller that a performing arts center would make the perfect addition to Saratoga and could be placed in Saratoga Spa State Park (see below). Rockefeller was enthusiastic and, on June 30, 1964, the official ground-breaking ceremonies took place. The Saratoga Performing Arts Center was completed two years later. Since then it has become one of the major summer festival sites in the nation, each year serving as summer home for the New York City Ballet (July) and the Philadelphia Orchestra (August). In addition, SPAC also has a Little Theatre seating 500. And, from June to September, SPAC presents popular entertainers ranging from Linda Ronstadt and Liberace to the Preservation Hall Jazz Band. This enormously successful formula now attracts more than 450,000 people during the season.

The amphitheater that houses the two major companies lies at the base of a gentle hill. It covers 150,000 square feet and can seat more than 5,000. (The surrounding hillside can absorb thousands more.)

One of my favorite stories about SPAC was told me by a prime mover in getting the center off the ground, Mrs. Lillian Phipps, who also is prominent in the Saratoga racing world. The first time the Philadelphia Orchestra held a rehearsal, she said, Eugene Ormandy mounted the podium, tapped his baton to call the orchestra to order, and then gave the downbeat. After a few bars he stopped, cocked his head and waved over an assistant. "What's that noise?" he asked. The assistant looked puzzled. "That gurgling," Ormandy elaborated. "That's a stream behind the amphitheater, Maestro." "Stop it at once!" Ormandy ordered. Thousands of dollars later, the offending stream was silenced.

Saratoga Spa State Park   The park covers 2,200 acres and includes the Saratoga Performing Arts Center; the Lincoln and Roosevelt baths (the Washington Baths, at this writing, is being converted into a National Dance Hall of Fame); two golf courses, one with 18 holes; a swimming pool complex with an Olympic-sized pool that can accommodate thousands of people; plus tennis courts, bridle trails and picnic areas. (As for the baths, the Roosevelt is open all year, the Lincoln in summer only. It's wise to reserve at least a week in advance. Phone: 518-584-2000.)

In the early 1900's, so many millions of gallons of the precious waters were being withdrawn by companies who extracted the carbonic gases for carbonating beverages that the citizens of the town began to worry that they might eventually exhaust their major natural resource. So they petitioned the state legislature to create a Saratoga Springs Reservation, which the state did, eventually taking over most of the wells in the Springs.

Then, in 1929, Franklin D. Roosevelt, governor at the time, created a special commission to develop the spa and appointed financier Bernard Baruch as chairman. (Baruch was a particularly apt choice; his father, whom he adored, had long advocated that the spa be developed into a European-style health resort. Today his name is honored by the Simon Baruch Research Laboratory in the park.) Bernard Baruch was not used to doing things in a small way—neither, for that matter, was FDR—and so by 1935 he had created the vast park and spa pretty much as it looks today, including the Gideon Putnam Hotel, now the finest in Saratoga.

Yaddo   Of all the glories of Saratoga, this certainly ranks among the most honorable.

In 1881, Spencer Trask (1844–1909), a New York banker who had made a considerable fortune, and his wife Katrina (1853–1922) purchased several hundred acres just outside the village for a summer home. In 1893 the 55-room Victorian mansion that still stands there today was completed and the Trasks moved in. Then an extraordinary series of tragedies struck. The Trasks' eldest son had died some years before, but now they lost their two remaining children over a short period of time to diphtheria.

Devastated, Spencer and Kate Trask planned to sell the estate, but then changed their minds and decided to leave it—and their entire fortune—to establish a retreat where artists, writers and musicians would be invited to work free from all distractions. Yaddo, as it is today, opened in 1926, four years after Kate Trask's death, and has been a monumental success ever since, harboring at various times such members of the American cultural hierarchy as John Cheever, Aaron Copland, Eudora Welty, Truman Capote, Philip Roth, Milton Avery and Leonard Bernstein. The public can visit the rose gardens, and the estate grounds are so lovely that it is worth taking the extra time to see them. (The entrance is on Union Avenue, about two miles southeast of the village.)

A Saratoga Walking Tour   The Springs is not only a treasure trove of Victorian architecture but contains fine examples from other periods, too. You should plan on spending some time in just wandering about. North Broadway, for instance, is still a prime street for the great racing families and has house after wonderful house to enjoy. You should certainly see Union Avenue, a wide, formal thoroughfare, with its mansions. Then there's Circular Street, with my favorite Victorian architectural fantasy, the 1873 Batcheller Mansion at No. 20. I'm also very fond of Franklin Square (take Division Street off Broadway) with its handsome Greek Revival homes. In addition, there are many antique shops in the area, and while you're wandering, you may want to stop in at the **Museum of Antiques and Art of Saratoga Springs (MAASS)** at 153 Regent Street, which is just off Union Avenue in the downtown area. Thirty dealers cover 9,000 square feet offering a very wide range of antiques. (Open all year 10–5 daily, 10–9 during August.)

Finally, for an overall impression of the town and what it has to offer, take the **Saratoga Circuit Tour**, a two-hour bus jaunt that will provide an excellent introduction to what you can later return to at your leisure. (June, weekends only, tours at 10 A.M.; July and August, daily tours at 10 A.M. and 1 P.M. Phone: 518-587-3656.)

Saratoga, renowned for its Victorian buildings, can also boast of some re-markably handsome homes from earlier in the nineteenth century.

Skidmore College   Founded in 1903 by Lucy Skidmore Scribner, the wife of publisher Charles Scribner, the college has now moved to a new 1,200-acre campus off North Broadway.

Saratoga Lake   Three miles east of the village, on Route 9P, Saratoga Lake offers boating, swimming, picnicking and amusement rides in summer, ice-skating and skiing in winter.

Saratoga Harness Racing   Open throughout most of the year. Call 518-584-2110 for exact schedule and times of events.

Environs of Saratoga Springs

The Hyde Collection   Located at 161 Warren Street in Glens Falls, 15 miles north of Saratoga Springs, this little museum in the former home of its donors, Louis Fiske and Charlotte Pruyn Hyde, is definitely worth a detour. The building is attractive, in the style of a Florentine Renaissance villa, and the collection, works ranging from the fourteenth into the twentieth century,

includes such names as Picasso, Matisse, Ingres, Rubens, Van
Dyck, Renoir, della Robbia (both Luca and Andrea), Raphael,
Tintoretto, Turner, Winslow Homer, Whistler and George Bel-
lows. (Open daily 12–5, except Mondays. Closed January and all
national holidays. Phone: 518-792-1761. Admission: $2; senior
citizens and students, $1.)

An Interesting Drive in Saratoga County and Nearby

This drive is among the most important, historically, in the
Hudson Valley. It also offers long stretches of serene mountain
beauty, a dreamland of timeless scenery, and enough diversity
to satisfy the most avid tourist. I particularly like to take it in
the fall; all of the "leaf people" are out in full cry—but mostly
in nearby Vermont and, consequently, I can enjoy basically the
same beautiful colors and scenery at my own leisurely pace
here. On the other hand, if it's your first time, I suggest your
doing it in the summer when everything along the route is open
to the public.

Start from Broadway, right in the center of Saratoga, after a
fortifying breakfast at **Mrs. London's Bake Shop** (see page 72).
I also would suggest that you take along a picnic basket as there
are no good restaurants to stop at for lunch on this trip. In any
case, turn from Broadway onto Route 29 East. This will take you
through the outskirts of the town and then you will be out in
flat, uninteresting countryside. Not to worry. Soon enough
the landscape will gently, almost imperceptibly, turn hilly,
with pines and clumps of woods and pretty farms to delight the
eye.

After 12 miles you will see the **Saratoga Battle Monument**
off to your right, and a sign will direct you to turn here to
approach it. This 155-foot granite memorial, completed in 1883,
could only have been created in the high Victorian era—it combines wildly disparate Gothic and Egyptian elements fighting
for your attention, but time has somehow made it endearing
and touching rather than grandiose—and was built to com-
memorate the surrender of the British commander, General
John Burgoyne, to General Horatio Gates on October 17, 1777.

It makes a perfect introduction to the whole **Saratoga National Park**, site of the historic Revolutionary battle that marked the turning point of the war. The monument stands on a summit 300 feet high, right where Burgoyne had his camp, and from its top you can take in a good part of the surrounding Hudson Valley and the flats where the surrender took place. The three statues in the outside niches, by the way, represent General Philip Schuyler (east), commander of the American forces during much of Burgoyne's campaign, General Horatio Gates (north), and Colonel Daniel Morgan (west) who led the famous Sharpshooters. On the south the niche is vacant, in symbolic tribute to Benedict Arnold, the fourth commander, who helped carry the victory but later became a traitor to the American cause, a course of action that may have begun right here, as you will see. (Open Memorial Day to Labor Day, daily 9–5. Admission: Free.)

Continue down the road that brought you to the monument and you will come into **Schuylerville**, right on the banks of the Hudson, where you will turn right on combined Routes 4, 32 and 29. This was the original town of Saratoga, and it was called Old Saratoga until 1831. By 1702 the Schuyler family had an estate here, and in 1763 Philip Schuyler, the general-to-be, began to develop his property, building the first linen mill in America, among other things; the settlement prospered and grew until Burgoyne and his army approached in 1777, causing a mass exodus.

In late summer the entwined scents of new-mown grass and stacked bales of hay perfume the air and have the same yearning appeal as the Sirens' call to Ulysses' men.

Today the **Schuyler House** is owned and run by the National Park Service and is on your left just as you cross the bridge leaving the village proper. (Open daily, Memorial Day to Labor Day. Admission: free. Phone: 518-695-3664.) Rebuilt by Philip Schuyler after the British burned it to the ground during the Saratoga campaign, it's a simple colonial house, though large enough for its time, that provides an interesting insight into local history and further information on the life of Schuyler, but it is by no means as important as Schuyler's town house in Albany (see page 38).

From here you continue south for about 8 miles to the entrance of the battlefield area itself, and this is a fascinating visit. To tell the truth, I'm not a person who finds it enthralling to examine in detail the various sites of ancient campaigns—I find the maneuvering of the different armies well beyond my comprehension—but this one is extremely well presented, quite clear in the way it is set forth, and stretches out over countryside that is subtly and undeniably lovely.

You should first go to the **Visitor Center** and museum, located on top of Fraser Hill and offering an extensive view of the surrounding landscape that gives you an overall idea of what you will later on see in detail. The museum part of the center has a small but well-chosen selection of articles, clothing, maps and other historical material connected with the campaign, but the most important thing here is a short (around 20 minutes) film, narrated by Burgess Meredith, that explains the progress of the whole campaign in simple, clear language. After this you're ready for the 9-mile drive, which the Park Service says will take four hours but which I say is nonsense unless you plan to stop and study carefully each of the 10 stops along the route as well as listen to the recorded dialogue at each. I suggest that you plan on an hour, two at the most. First, though, an explanation of the campaign and what it meant to the course of the American Revolution.

The campaign was the idea of John Burgoyne, called "Gentleman Johnny" by his admiring troops, who convinced the political powers in England that the capture of the Lake Champlain–Hudson River waterways would split the colonies in two, allowing the British to pick up the remaining pieces at their leisure. This was not a new idea; throughout the colonial

period this route had been fought over by everyone from the
Indians to the French as the most important "highway,"
strategically and economically, in America.

As Burgoyne wrote, "I have always thought Hudson's River
the most proper part of the whole continent for opening vigorous operations. Because the course of the river, so beneficial for
conveying all the bulky necessities of any army, is precisely the
route that an army ought to take for the great purposes of
cutting the communications between the Southern and Northern provinces, giving confidence to the Indians and securing a
junction with the Canadian forces. These purposes effected, and
a fleet upon the coast, it is to me morally certain that the forces
of New England must be reduced so early in the campaign to
give you battle upon your own terms, or perish before the end
of it for want of necessary supplies."

Burgoyne's general plan was to sweep south from Canada,
advancing to Albany, where he would then link up with General
Sir William Howe, who had captured New York City in 1776 and
would now advance from there up the Hudson.

Howe, though, had other ideas. He was more in favor of a
campaign in Pennsylvania to capture Philadelphia, ultimately
choosing a sea-route invasion via the Chesapeake Bay. This
decision had disastrous results from Burgoyne's point of view
because, for various reasons, it delayed the British from starting north from New York until October 3, 1777, and because it
allowed General Washington to send men northward without
having to worry any longer about the main force of British
troops. In retrospect, Howe just didn't seem too interested in
this invasion from the north and abandoned it before it was well
under way.

In the meantime, Burgoyne was making a brave start with
his 8,000-man army, moving south from the St. Lawrence at the
beginning of June 1777. At first all went well, the army taking
Crown Point, 10 miles north of Fort Ticonderoga, easily enough,
and then moving on Ticonderoga itself, which commanded the
southern end of Lake Champlain and Lake George and was held
by a small number of troops under the American Major General
Arthur St. Clair. The fort fell to the British on July 6.

By mid-July Burgoyne was at Fort Edward. In early August
he heard that the Americans had a supply depot at Bennington,

Vermont, that would, if captured, solve the problem of his dangerously lengthening supply lines. He promptly sent off troops to capture it. They never even reached the Vermont border. General John Stark and 1,500 of his New Hampshire Green Mountain Boys met the advancing British a few miles west of Bennington. On August 16, they roundly defeated them, killing or capturing more than 900 British soldiers. This defeat, important in itself, of course, also gave a great boost to American morale when it was most desperately needed and helped to bring hundreds of volunteers to General Horatio Gates, who took command of the American army from General Schuyler on August 19. (Another British failure at this same time, on the Mohawk River at Fort Stanwix, caused the loss to Burgoyne of fresh troops coming from Canada who were to join him in Albany.)

Not at all daunted, Burgoyne marched south and crossed to the west bank of the Hudson, where American actions slowed his progress to about a mile a day. By now it was early September and Gates had evolved his own strategy: He moved his troops to Bemis Heights, near Old Saratoga and above the Hudson just where the river turns and forces the Albany road to go along the base of the commanding bluffs. Here Gates waited, with an army that now outnumbered Burgoyne's by about 2,000 men.

On September 19 Burgoyne made his decision; he would attack and force his way through to Albany. The battle raged on all day, but Burgoyne was unable to achieve his objective and thereby lost this round while handing the Americans an important victory.

(Benedict Arnold particularly distinguished himself and was furious when Gates failed to single him out in his report to Congress. Some say jealousy was the motive. Whatever the reason, a quarrel developed that led to Gates' removing Arnold of his command—and that in turn probably planted the first seeds of treasonable thoughts in Arnold's vain and extremely proud head.)

For more than two weeks now the armies warily faced each other without giving further fight, but the British position was growing weaker by the day. On September 21, they learned that retreat to Canada had been cut off by troops under General

Benjamin Lincoln who had retaken the outworks at Fort Ticonderoga. On October 4 rations were reduced. And over all loomed
the threat of the oncoming and, especially for the footsore and
weary British, devastating weather of an Adirondack fall and
winter.

On October 7 Burgoyne took a gamble and attacked. Once
again he failed. It was all over, but still he refused to surrender.
Instead, he began to retreat. On the 11th he ordered the buildings on the Schuyler estate to be burned, by now a useless act
of destruction. Finally, on October 17, he capitulated and formally surrendered, the first such action by a British army commander on American soil.

The battle of Saratoga was an extremely important victory
for the Americans, one that strongly influenced the entire
course of the war. Among other things, it convinced France, at
last, to openly join the American side, an event that helped
ensure our ultimate victory at Yorktown.

Enough history. Now you're ready for the drive through the
battlefield itself. Each stop along the route has its own recorded
narration explaining what happened there; stop and listen as
you choose. I would suggest, though, that you do visit at least
a few of these sites if only because the surrounding countryside
and the views are so lovely—the land is mostly open here so you
can often see for miles to the mountains in Vermont—and the
narration is remarkably good. And then it's quite pleasant to
walk along any of the numerous trails, sometimes surprising
grazing deer (if you're lucky) and just generally enjoying yourself.

I do have a few favorite stops. I particularly like the Revolutionary monuments—one put up by the Poles to honor
Tadeusz Kosciuszko who built the trenches, another to the
Unknown Soldier, yet another to Colonel Daniel Morgan,
whose Rifle Corps was so important to the American success,
this one erected by a descendant—all of which are simple and
have a calm dignity that brings you closer in human terms to
the actual meaning of the battles than any history book possibly could. I suppose my favorite stop of all, though, is near the
end of the drive where you can get out of your car and look
down on the Hudson, smallish and unimpressive here, and
then suddenly you realize how central this river is to our his-

tory—and it doesn't look so unimpressive after all. (Tour roads are open from April 15 through November, weather permitting. The park itself is open daily, 9–5. Closed January 1, Thanksgiving and Christmas day. Admission: Free. Phone: 518-664-9821.)

When you leave the park, turn left and, after about 500 feet, you will see a sign on your right for River Road. Take it. For about two miles it runs along the banks of the river and the houses alongside have little docks for their speedboats. Who from New York City or lower on the Hudson would believe it? There's even a small farm with cows grazing on the bank, for all the world a seventeenth-century Dutch landscape transported out of time.

At the end you will rejoin the highway and go back into Schuylerville. Here you will turn right on Route 29 East and, once across the river, stay on 29 to **Greenwich**, where you will get on 372. (If you have time, explore Greenwich; it has some stunning houses.)

Once you leave Greenwich you will find yourself in unspoiled country that is entrancing for its rapidly changing views of hills and valleys, handsome farms and general aura of undisturbed tranquillity. It is a nineteenth-century version of the Peaceable Kingdom come to life. This wonderful road will eventually bring you into **Cambridge**, but if you have the time, turn right at the sign for Center Cambridge and drive for a while, drinking it all in.

Cambridge is a charming, totally unspoiled village—you're in Grandma Moses country here; her hometown of Hoosick Falls is only a few miles farther south. There are a few antique shops on the main street, nothing special, but this gives you a nice excuse to walk around, and they're fun to look through. Then continue on to the traffic light and go straight. Next is a Stop sign. Go straight again, and you are on County Route 67. This will take you, in a few miles, to a sign for the singular monastery of the **Monks of New Skete**. This Russian Orthodox monastery has a small, beautiful church with gold-leaf onion domes; inside are darkly glowing icons. It seems strange to come across such a place of worship in this so-American setting, but for that very reason it is well worth a visit. The monks also operate a gift shop on the grounds with, in particu-

The golden onion domes of the Russian church at the Monastery of New Skete, a startling yet somehow appropriate apparition in a basically New England landscape.

lar, handsome icons as well as some delicious foodstuffs for sale. (They also run a dog obedience training school that has become famous; they even trained the dog of exiled Russian novelist Aleksandr Solzhenitsyn in Russian. For information and a catalogue of their offerings, phone: 518-677-3928, or write: Monks of New Skete, Cambridge, N.Y. 12816.) Nearby are the Sisters of New Skete, whose gift shop offers a sinfully delicious chocolate cheesecake.

ALBANY COUNTY

Albany

For its size, and despite what you may have heard about it, Albany is a surprisingly interesting city. A pleasant old Dutch town in the nineteenth century—"Antique Albany," Henry James called it; his grandfather made the family fortune there and he always had a soft spot in his heart for the city—it was definitely on the skids by the time World War II ended. It still remains the butt of gibes and jokes, in much the same way as W. C. Fields thought of Philadelphia. But, also like Philadelphia, people were laughing so hard at all the jokes they didn't notice that the city has suddenly been revived and is blossoming. The Empire State Plaza, for one example, has had a genuine revitalizing effect on Albany's downtown core, and many of the down-and-out city blocks are being reborn as handsome urban dwelling areas as people buy and restore the houses. But there's more, much more, than that. Albany, as you'll see, has a lot to offer.

HISTORY

With a population of slightly more than 100,000, Albany wouldn't exist without the Hudson. It lies at the head of the navigable part of the river, about 145 miles from the Atlantic Ocean, and is, after New York City, the river's greatest port and this country's sixth largest.

It is possible that French traders were trafficking with Indians here well before Henry Hudson sailed up the river in 1609. But it was his "discovery" that gave impetus to settling the area, which was accomplished by 1614, making it the second oldest permanent settlement in the original thirteen colonies. The reason for this interest on the part of the Dutch: Beaver and other skins were brought here by the Indians from as far distant as Lake Superior over the ancient Iroquois trail, and the Dutch West India Company could smell the potential profits all the way from Amsterdam. (The Dutch West India Company, which operated from 1621 to 1791, was chartered by the Dutch Government and controlled all trade in New York—or New Netherland—until the English conquered the colony in 1664.)

In 1629, the Dutch West India Company came up with an idea to gain more stability for the settlement, then known as Fort Orange. This was a new version of the feudal manorial concept that became known as the patroon system, the patroon being the lord of the manor. Very briefly, it meant that extensive land and manorial privileges would be granted to the patroon for settling a colony of 50 or more people.

The family that became most famous as patroons were the Van Rensselaers, and their first patroon was Kiliaen. By the mid-seventeenth century, this patroonship—called Rensselaerswyck—was so vast that it extended over 700,000 acres and included what today is Albany County as well as parts of Columbia and Rensselaer counties. The tenants on Kiliaen Van Rensselaer's lands—immigrants and settlers—were required, among other duties, to give him one third of their crops in rent. When the English arrived they continued the system, and it wasn't until the 1840's that it finally ended. The last patroon, Stephen Van Rensselaer III, known as Stephen III, founded Rensselaer Polytechnic Institute (1824) and also played a key role in the development of the Albany Institute (see page 35). When he died in 1839, Stephen III's heirs tried to realize the monies owed the estate—about $400,000, an enormous fortune at the time—in uncollected rents. Open resistance followed, involving land tenants as far south as the town of Hudson, and the whole affair became known as the Rent Wars. Finally, in 1846, the state outlawed the feudal practice of land-lease that could claim rent or service. Samuel Eliot Morison, in his *Oxford History of the American People,* points out that this system made New York the most aristocratic of the colonies and caused it to be the most Tory of the thirteen during the Revolution.

The settlement prospered on its fur trade, and the only change the English instituted when they captured the colony was to change its name of Fort Orange to Albany in honor of its new proprietor, James, duke of Albany and of York and later James II, king of England. In 1686 Albany was chartered as a city—after settling the Van Rensselaers' claims to owning the place outright—and from then until the Revolution it slowly grew, with agriculture eventually replacing the fur trade.

Once independence was gained, the city entered into a new era and, thanks to its excellent turnpike system and central location, quickly became the gateway to the West for New Englanders as well as capital of the state in 1797. Then, with the completion of the Erie Canal in 1825, linking Lake Erie and the other Great Lakes with the Hudson and the Atlantic Ocean, the city boomed, its population doubling in a few years. And, as the railroads developed, Albany became a nerve center for this form of transportation, too, tying together the Northeast with the rapidly expanding West. By the mid-nineteenth century, Albany was a major link between east and west and the financial center of upstate New York, two positions the city still holds today.

As I mentioned at the start of this section, Albany fell on hard times after World War II when the population moved out to the suburbs and began avoiding downtown for the more convenient malls. Unlike other cities, though, Albany got Nelson Rockefeller as resident governor, and he soon decided he was going to convert this sow's ear into a magnificent silk purse. In fact, he repeatedly said that his plans would make Albany one of the most beautiful capitals in the world.

What to See and Do

The Nelson A. Rockefeller Empire State Plaza (The Mall)

In 1959, as part of the celebration of the 350th anniversary of Henry Hudson's discovery of the Hudson, Governor Rockefeller received Princess Beatrix of the Netherlands in Albany. Driving her to the Executive Mansion, he was so embarrassed by the tawdriness of their surroundings that he decided, then and there, that the city must be revitalized—and thus the concept for the Mall was born.

It makes a wonderful story, and it *is* true that the governor was mortified every time an important visitor came to Albany

Albany's famous (or infamous) Mall, with the State Capitol at the end. To the right is the Egg. The false story—but accurate description—is that Nelson Rockefeller designed it by placing a grapefruit half on a container of cream.

—but contrary to what you may be told, this was only one factor in Rockefeller's decision to build the Mall. Long before that, he'd been wrestling with the problem of a severe shortage of office space for state government employees. And then, of course, there was his own family's precedent: back in the thirties, Rockefeller Center in New York City had shown what could be brilliantly done to revitalize a dying urban core.

Rockefeller and his aides decided that the present site was ideal because, first, it would allow them to incorporate the old Capitol Building in their plans; and second, the 98.5 acres probably could be had at a reasonable overall price. In July 1962 the project, soon to develop into one of the largest and most expensive ($2 billion) in history, began.

Rockefeller's choice for the chief architect was Wallace K. Harrison, who had been deeply involved in the creation of Rockefeller Center, the United Nations headquarters and, at the same time he was working on the Mall, the development of Lincoln Center, all in New York City. All were pet projects of the Rockefeller family, and Harrison had been close to Nelson, in particular, for years.

On a plane from New York to Washington the governor told Harrison what he wanted, outlining his ideas on the back of a postcard. In the main area, the Mall would consist of four small office buildings based on a skyscraper design Harrison had never yet realized but that had fascinated Rockefeller for years; the plan is distinguished by the fact that each building is "held" by a 23-story "clamp" that contains the elevator shafts and building services. There also would be a 44-story office tower, the tallest in the state outside Manhattan, a convention center, the Legislative Office and Justice buildings and the Swan Street Building—the latter structure a quarter of a mile long. (The State Museum Library and the Performing Arts Center—The Egg—would come later.) All of these buildings would be placed on an immense platform consisting of five stories that would be a quarter of a mile long and an eighth of a mile wide, making the platform itself one of the largest structures in the world. This would serve not only as protection from Albany's notorious winters but would also contain dozens of shops and the Mall's collection of contemporary paintings. It was Rockefeller, too, who wanted the north-south wall, the Mall's best feature and so striking when seen from the city below; his inspiration came from the monastery walls he had been so impressed by in Tibet.

From the beginning the project was plagued with problems: delays, cost overruns, strikes . . . you name it. Finally in 1978, with the completion of The Egg, the Mall was done. Years behind schedule, true, and hundreds of millions of dollars more than the original published estimates, but there it finally sat. So what, in fact, did the State of New York get for those two billion dollars?

Aesthetically, I don't find the Mall all that interesting in its parts. The four Agency buildings, with the C-clamp configuration Rockefeller so admired, are minimally effective and then only through repetition. The office tower is banal. The five-block-long Sawn Street Building is not only in harsh contrast to the surrounding residential neighborhood but totally boring in execution as well. The Egg, supposedly designed to provide an effective counter-poise to the strong verticals and horizontals of the other buildings, is, instead, lumpish and faintly threatening. There is a story that Rockefeller designed the building by placing a grapefruit half over a container of cream. It's not true, but it's also not a bad description of what he got. The Justice, Legislative Office and Museum Library buildings are completely undistinguished. The Museum Library is particularly irritating to me; the grand staircase leading up to it usually can't even be used to gain access to the building—the doors are kept locked. Supposedly, Harrison thought this was his best contribution to the Mall, but it's only ponderous.

Still, the Mall has had an undeniably beneficial impact on Albany; the surrounding houses and office buildings are being carefully and beautifully restored and the plaza itself is in constant use, providing an extremely welcome oasis in this grimly urban setting. One nice touch—the steps in front of the Museum Library may lead nowhere, but they can and do serve as bleachers for concerts and other events on the plaza. The overall problem is that the plaza is not a welcoming space. It's handsome enough with its trees and pools, but it's just too big and official-looking. Has it turned Albany into one of the most striking capitals as Rockefeller envisioned? Could be. It is unique and vast and monumental and severe and striking and many other things. But it is not beautiful.

The single most interesting aspect of the Mall—and certainly a prime reason for you to explore it—is the **art collection** that Rockefeller had the state buy and place here during the 1960's. Originally, all the works of art included were to have been created by New York artists, and most of them still do meet this criterion. Today there are 92 paintings and sculptures in a collection that cost just under $2 million. The sculptures are scattered about the plaza and on the Concourse below. The paintings are along the Concourse. Some of the legendary names you will encounter: Alexander Calder, Adolph Gottlieb, Helen Frankenthaler, Philip Guston, Isamu Noguchi, Robert Motherwell, David Smith, Louise Nevelson, Claes Oldenburg. The collection constitutes a magnificent retrospective of our art at a particularly vibrant time in its history. (Tours in front of Visitors Services every Wednesday at 10:30 A.M. and 2:30 P.M. By reservation, seven days a week. Admission: Free. Phone: 518-473-7521.)

You should also go up to the Tower Building Observation deck from which you can see for miles. (Daily, 9–4. Closed January 1, Thanksgiving and Christmas day. Admission: Free. Phone: 518-474-2418.) The **Museum** is fun, too, particularly for kids. Three major permanent displays are planned; two—New York Metropolis and Adirondack Wilderness—are already on view. The third, Upstate New York, is scheduled to open soon. The Museum also offers a dozen changing exhibits each year.

The overall idea of these displays is to recreate aspects of life at different times and places in the state, and this is so beautifully accomplished that the Museum has already become a major tourist attraction. In the Adirondack Wilderness section, ranging in time from 4,000 years ago to today, you hear a blue jay calling from a tree, watch old films of the great logging days, and wander through exhibits covering everything from camping and fishing to Adirondack resort history to models of animals and birds in their natural habitats. In the New York Metropolis exhibit, my own favorite, you can see a replica of a tenement sweat shop or explore a 1940's version of a subway car or peer at people dining in turn-of-the-century Delmonico's or study old fire engines. Both exhibits are a cornucopia of life in New York State, and many of the visual displays are supplemented by award-winning films and/or narration. Give yourself at least two hours to thoroughly enjoy it all. Within the Museum, too, is an excellent book and gift shop with an outstanding collection of books on New York State. (The Museum is open daily, 10–5, except on January 1, Thanksgiving and Christmas Day. Admission: Free. Phone: 518-474-5877.)

If you would like to see the Mall in more detail, tours are available daily. (Free. Phone for times: 518-474-2418.)

The State Capitol If the Mall is formed of straight lines, vertical and horizontal, the Capitol is all exuberant curves, angles and disparate styles and, thankfully, very much in joyous contrast to its neighbor. It is an immense relief, after trudging through the Mall, to come upon the old Capitol, quaint and cozy by comparison, and a fascinating building to visit. Nevertheless, the two complexes do have a couple of things in common; in particular, they both took forever to build (1867–98 for the Capitol) and both involved immense outlays of money. Two staircases, the Great Western and the Eastern Approach, cost well over $1 million *each,* and the whole structure exceeded $25 million, far more than any other capitol building in the nation and twice as much as the one in Washington. By the way, it is also one of the few capitols without a dome.

The history of the building is a saga in itself. The first architect to become involved was Thomas Fuller, responsible for the Gothic parliament buildings in Ottawa. Fuller was chosen by the state to erect his winning design for an edifice that was essentially Italian Renaissance in style. He went energetically to work but, by 1876, had managed to spend a great deal more money than anyone had anticipated, and besides, somewhat belatedly, the legislature decided they didn't like his plans for the interior. Out he went.

In came Leopold Eidlitz and Henry Hobson Richardson. Here the story takes on a more Byzantine complexity. Eidlitz, an immigrant from Prague, loved anything Gothic and also had a passion for the Near Eastern approach to ornament, in particular a mélange of Moorish and Saracen elements. One of his more astounding contributions along these lines was P. T. Barnum's house in Bridgeport, Connecticut, called, aptly enough, "Iranistan."

The Great Western Staircase in the Capitol. Designed by H. H. Richardson, it offers a seeming infinity of magnificent stone carvings quite fascinating to explore.

Richardson, who would die in 1886 at the age of forty-eight before the building was completed, was one of the great architects in American history. His masterpiece is Trinity Church in Boston, but he also built City Hall in Albany, just across the park from the Capitol. Richardson was particularly fond of the Romanesque style and adapted its forms and principles to his own highly idiosyncratic approach. Both Charles McKim and Stanford White worked with him (see page 115) and, later, Frank Lloyd Wright studied Richardson's buildings with great care.

But on with the story. By the time these two men were chosen, the first two floors of the building had been completed—in grandiose Italian Renaissance style. Not at all disconcerted, they drew up their own, totally different plans for the remaining three stories—and somehow got them approved. So what you see today is practically a short-order history of architecture in one single building. The first two floors are Italian Renaissance, as noted; the third is some kind of hybrid transitional to the fourth, which is Romanesque; and the fifth is French Renaissance. To read about it beforehand is to expect architectural anarchy, I grant you, but take a close look at it: somehow it does all come together and emerges a unified whole.

Wisely, considering their differing tastes, Eidlitz and Richardson divided the interior between them; Eidlitz, for instance, took the Assembly Chamber and the Senate Staircase, Richardson the Senate Chamber and the Great Western Staircase, called now "the million-dollar staircase" even though it cost half again as much.

The Senate Chamber has been termed the most beautiful legislative hall in this country. That may be taking it a bit too far, but it is a remarkable tour de force and shouldn't be missed. A large sum of money was appropriated for its decoration, and Richardson was just the man to spend it. Consider his materials and colors: golden onyx from Mexico, rich brown mahogany from the Caribbean, deep red leather for the chairs and for some of the paneling, gold leaf and yellow sienna marble, red granite and pink marble and stained glass. The effect isn't dazzling—the colors are too soft—but there is a warmth and opulence and overall masculinity well-suited (at the time, anyway) to the highest legislative body of the Empire State. For once the legislators got what they paid for. Richardson even designed the furniture, including the extremely handsome tall-case clock you see to the right front of the chamber. As for the massive fireplaces, they were to have been engraved according to sketches by Stanford White, who was working with Richardson at that time; unfortunately, these were never executed. Even so, the chamber remains formidably impressive, especially now that it has been completely restored to its original splendors, and visiting it is an enlightening experience. Maybe it *is* the handsomest legislative chamber after all.

Other than this chamber, the most interesting parts of the interior are the Senate Staircase and the Great Western Staircase. For the Senate Staircase, Eidlitz decided to indulge his passion for the Gothic including, bizarrely enough, a rose window form set within the staircase itself. It definitely does not work. Far more amusing was another idea of Eidlitz's: to illustrate Darwin's theory of evolution in carved stone on the arabesques that border the stairs from the bottom to the top. At the bottom are forms of sea life to begin the scale—no figure is repeated, by the way—and at the very top are an elephant and a camel. Eidlitz had to do this all on the sly, of course, as the theory was still highly controversial and his plan would never have been approved by the legislators. It works wonderfully, the carvings are extremely well done, and the progression of life forms gives the staircase a sense of "flow" it would otherwise lack.

The Great Western Staircase is another Richardson extravaganza. The stairwell measures 77 by 70 feet and from floor to skylight the distance is 119 feet. It was begun in 1884, structurally completed in 1897, but the last figures weren't carved until 1898. As I mentioned earlier, it cost about $1.5 million to complete. So much for statistics. The fact is that you could look at it for hours on end and still not see it all because of the near fantastical number of carvings that, vine-like, decorate so much of the surfaces. Most of the heads are historical—there, for one, is James Fenimore Cooper, surrounded by characters from his *Leatherstocking Tales,* while around the corner Civil War Major General Winfield Scott Hancock looks bravely out at the world. Harriet Beecher Stowe may be smiling, but Susan B. Anthony is definitely not amused. In the "Poet's Corner" Walt Whitman barely emerges from the surrounding foliage, while William Cullen Bryant stares heavenward in a confident manner. Washington is there, of course, and Hamilton and Franklin and Lincoln and Grant. On and on it goes, a veritable national portrait gallery in stone, a delight to the eye and to the senses and a magnificent tribute to the dying art of the stone carver. One sad note: During World War II, the skylight that allowed the staircase to be flooded with light was covered up and hasn't yet been restored. The lighting, therefore, is not the best.

The stone carvers—at one time more than 600 cutters and

carvers worked on the building—were given one other magnificent project, the Eastern Approach staircase on the front of the
Capitol. Here the carvings are either generally symbolic (a
farmer, a freed slave), or of animals and birds and flowers (an
owl, raccoon, bison, roses, clematis), or else idealized concepts—
Plenty (feminine) and Progress (male) stand guard over the
entrances to the porte-cochere, for example, the two most elaborate carvings on the entire building. And, once again, you can
spend as much time as you like exploring the staircase without
ever exhausting its possibilities.

It is, yes, a unique building—one you may or may not like, but
it certainly is worth seeing once. (Guided tours daily on the hour
9–4 except on January 1, Thanksgiving and Christmas Day.
Admission: Free. Phone: 518-474-2418.)

The Albany Institute of History and Art   The Institute is a
great rarity, a brilliant, many-faceted gem of a regional museum that, since this area was extremely rich and diversified in
its art of the eighteenth and nineteenth centuries, has been able
to amass collections which go beyond the strictly regional to
form part of the mainstream of our national cultural heritage.
There is much here that's vital to any understanding of how
American art developed. In particular I'm thinking of the Institute's extensive holdings in folk art, its canvases of the Hudson
River School, and various exhibits of New York furniture and
silver. If any of these interest you a visit here is all but imperative.

Although a forerunner of the present Institute opened in
1791, making it one of the oldest museums in the country, it
wasn't until 1824, with the merger of the Albany Lyceum of
Natural History and the Society for the Promotion of Useful
Arts, that the present organization began to take shape. Then,
in 1898, the Albany Gallery of Fine Arts was added and finally
the revised and expanded society moved into its current quarters in 1907. In 1926 its present title was adopted and today,
according to its bylaws, the Institute's goal is to acquire and
preserve "significant historical materials and superior works of
art and artifacts pertinent to the past and present culture of the
City of Albany and the upper Hudson region." (The Institute is
not, however, exclusively regional or even American. On the

second floor, to your right, is a collection of eighteenth-century English porcelains, furniture and portraits set out in three small but charming rooms, one of which has paneling from an early eighteenth-century London house.)

The collections are on three smallish floors, and to describe them in detail would overload you with information you don't need. Suffice it to say that the Hudson River School collection includes superb examples by Thomas Cole, Asher B. Durand, John F. Kensett and Jasper Cropsey, to drop only a few names. As for the folk art canvases from the nineteenth century, almost every one is top drawer and you'll probably come across several that seem strangely familiar—for they are often reproduced in books and on posters as prime examples of Americana.

Instead, I'd rather tell you about one small, unique room that could change your perceptions of American art and its achievements before 1800. First, go the second floor and look at the restored Dutch room to your left; it's very well arranged and contains one or two choice pieces of Hudson Valley Dutch furniture, such as the *Kas* (chest) that belonged to the wife of a Van Rensselaer. Then move on to the neighboring Dutch gallery. Here you will see a collection of early American paintings that, in its size and overall quality, is without peer.

Done, basically, between 1700 and 1750 in the Hudson River Valley, this group of canvases, mostly by anonymous artists, represents the first significant work by any group of painters in this country. To see so many of them together is overwhelming, but a description of only three should give you some idea of what to expect.

My favorite is the life-size, full-length portrait of Ariaantje Coeymans (Mrs. David Ver Planck), painted about 1717 and attributed to "the Schuyler limner." ("Limner" is the generic term used to describe the untrained and unknown painters of colonial America.) This lady was born in Albany in 1672 to a Dutch émigré father who proceeded to make a fortune and owned a great deal of land in the area. Ariaantje married Ver Planck at the age of fifty-one—he was only twenty-eight—and died in 1743 at what was then considered the ripe old age of seventy-one.

In this portrait Ariaantje seems encased in her no-nonsense steel-gray dress with its black and brown trim and stiff, symmetrical folds. Her feet, large and ungainly, look more like balancing supports than part of her body, and in her outstretched hand she holds a red rose. Her face, though, is wonderful—not beautiful, but strong and filled with character and life, while her eyes and slight smile indicate a woman of high intelligence and no little humor as she looks out at the viewer inviting him to share her pleasure. The background, an Italianate view in shades of pink, has been traced to a mezzotint of Lady Bucknell (c. 1686) after Sir Godfrey Kneller, although here it has been greatly changed. It was not unusual at this time for artists to use mezzotints after English portraits as inspiration for their backgrounds and poses. What makes this picture so breathtaking, though, is its overall impression of great strength and honesty. Awkward it may appear, but in its straightforwardness and independence in execution from contemporary European models this could only be an American painting.

The second canvas is completely different and is attributed to "Pieter Vanderlyn" (c. 1687–1778), grandfather of John (see page 84). (Pieter came to this country from Holland via Curaçao around 1718. He first lived in Albany, then Kingston.) It is a portrait from about 1725 of Pau de Wandelaer, son of a prosperous family who lived in both Albany and New York City. The colors are subdued and soft, browns and buffs, and the boy stands in front of us with an almost mystical expression, a small bird perched on one hand, the other thrust inside his shirt. The background, one of the first depictions of the Hudson, underscores the mystical feeling with its small sloop, lying empty and at anchor. There is a dreamy quality about the whole, a sort of fading vision of a primitive, childhood Eden that the boy is losing as he approaches manhood. It is a superior example of inner psychology given outward expression.

The third portrait is of Mrs. Petrus Vas and was probably painted by Gerardus Duyckinck (1695–1746). As in the Pau de Wandelaer portrait, the colors are muted—brown, blue, gray—but the overall effect is totally different. Mrs. Vas wears a gray-white shawl that sets off her long, elegant face as in a frame and whose ends fall almost to her waist. Seated, her exquisite hands relaxed and in full view, she neither questions nor demands; there is an aura of delicacy about this portrait that borders on the chaste. A woman of great refinement and depth, this Mrs.

Vas, who keeps a discreet distance between herself and the viewer yet whose eyes are so veiled with experience you keep going back to the picture to try and penetrate her secrets.

And these are only three of the paintings. It's an eye- and mind-opener, this gallery, and you owe it to yourself to see—and savor—it.

One other artist should be mentioned and that is Ezra Ames (1768–1836) whose paintings fill the entrance hallway and whose daughter married William James, the uncle of novelist Henry James and philosopher William James. (Her portrait, done by her father, is in the Institute collection.) Known as *the* portrait painter of Albany, Ames was not among the greatest of his day, but when he had an interesting subject he could catch his or her characteristics with a vigorous intelligence that makes him worthy of respect.

The Institute, located at 125 Washington Avenue, just a block west of the Capitol, also has a neighboring library with more of the collection on display and a superb library of regional reference books. The galleries are open Tuesday–Saturday 10–4:45, Sunday 2–5. Admission: Donation. The library is open Tuesday–Friday 9–3. There also is a luncheon gallery, open Tuesday–Friday 11:30–1:30. Study appointments for the collection can be made. Phone: 518-463-4478.

Historic Houses of Albany

Schuyler Mansion State Historic Site   Of all the historic houses in Albany this is by far the most interesting and beautiful. If you have time to visit only one, the Schuyler Mansion should definitely be your choice.

Philip John Schuyler, who built the house, was born on November 10, 1733, into an extremely prominent family who had first arrived in this country in 1650. He became a successful businessman himself and at one time was said to own 125,000 acres of land in the upper Hudson area. In 1755, Schuyler married Kitty Van Rensselaer of Fort Crailo (see page 40); he began to build the present house six years later. In 1761, during a trip to England, Schuyler bought vast amounts of goods for the house, which was nearing completion when he returned in 1762. In those days, it stood on 125 acres of land at the southern end of the city, high on a ridge, and offered lovely views of the Hudson and the Catskills far to the south, while 12 acres of lawns and gardens surrounded the building itself.

As the Revolution approached, Schuyler sided with the patriots and was named a delegate to the Continental Congress. A close friend of George Washington, he later was commissioned a major general in command of the Northern Department, an appointment that would become his grief, for he was removed —unjustly, most historians believe—just before the Battle of Saratoga (see page 17) and the major share of the glory for that victory went to General Gates. Schuyler was later exonerated completely of any wrongdoing. After the battle, the defeated General Burgoyne was Schuyler's guest for a time, and he also entertained Washington, Franklin and Lafayette, among others. In 1780, his daughter married Alexander Hamilton in the formal drawing room.

Schuyler led an active public life after the war and became a U.S. Senator in 1789. He died in 1804, and the mansion was sold out of the family. Finally, in 1912, the State of New York bought the house and began the restoration that you see today.

The Schuylers called their house "The Pastures," and today it remains one of the most beautiful Georgian houses in the state. Built of rose-red brick, its most striking features on the exterior are the double-hipped roof with its three dormer windows and a particularly exquisite Chinese-fret roof balustrade, and the hexagonal entrance vestibule, added much later (c. 1818) but giving the house a peculiar uniqueness that I enjoy, although architectural purists inevitably cringe when they see it.

Inside, the house is divided in half on each floor by a very wide and beautifully proportioned hallway, with two spacious rooms on each side. A few highlights here, just to give you a taste of the whole: The staircase, shipped from Boston, has three different balusters, beautifully carved, on each stair; the formal drawing room, where Hamilton was married, contains a magnificently ornamented chimney piece (mantelpiece, to us modern-day Americans) with a broken-scroll pediment and Philadelphia marble facings, not to mention superb ornamental carving throughout the room and a glittering chandelier that casts its light over satinwood Hepplewhite furniture. So it goes throughout the house. The times I have been there no other visitor has gone through the house with me, so it's a safe bet that you, too, will have it pretty much to yourself.

The house is at 32 Catharine Street, between Morton Avenue and Fourth Avenue, and is open Wednesday–Saturday 10–5, Sunday 1–5, from April to December. Admission: Free. For winter hours, it's advisable to phone: 518-474-3953. Closed holidays except Memorial Day, July 4 and Labor Day. There is also a well-made short film you can see before wandering through the house that should give you a good background on the Schuylers.

The Ten Broeck Mansion   My favorite story about this house took place in 1977. Someone happened to be exploring the old wine cellar and came across a cache of nearly 25 cases of Burgundies and Bordeaux that had been bottled in the 1870's and '80's. About half the bottles were intact and realized $45,000—one bottle sold for just under $3,000—at a special auction that drew wine connoisseurs to Albany like flies to honey. The proceeds went to such mundane projects as repairing the roof and installing a new furnace.

Like the Schuylers, the Ten Broecks were an old Albany family, the first Ten Broeck having arrived on these shores in 1626 with Peter Minuit, the first governor of New Netherland and the man who bought Manhattan for $24. One early Ten Broeck, namely Abraham, married Elizabeth Van Rensselaer (did a Van Rensselaer ever marry a bum?), grew increasingly prosperous, gained some renown for his leadership at the Battle of Saratoga and eventually went on to become mayor of Albany, a member of the State Senate and president of the city's first bank. Abraham built this mansion in 1798 after his first house had burned to the ground. In 1810 he died, and thirty-eight years later the house passed from the Ten Broecks into the hands of the Olcott family, one of whose members built the executive mansion (see page 41). The Olcotts lived in the house that Abraham built until 1947, when they gave it to the Albany County Historical Association.

The house is Federal on the exterior with a Georgian plan—four rooms to a floor—inside. Unfortunately, about 1850 some major architectural changes were made, and today the house is of only minor interest, although it contains some choice examples of Federal furniture. The house is located at 9 Ten Broeck Place and is open Tuesday–Saturday, 2–4, Sunday 1–4. Closed on holidays. Admission: Donation. Phone: 518-436-9826.

Historic Cherry Hill   If you never thought that a house could be crazed and boring while containing some beautiful things, check out Cherry Hill. Built in 1787, the house was originally part of a 900-acre farm that belonged to Philip Van Rensselaer. A pretty frame structure in the Georgian style, but extensively remodeled inside, it remained in this branch of the family until 1963 when the last member died and left it to the group that now operates it, Historic Cherry Hill.

The house is jammed to the rafters with some good—even superb—things and a whole lot of junk: Kerosene lamp collections and old kitchen utensils and dolls vie with excellent china examples and unique textiles. You get the idea. But there is one fascinating event connected with Cherry Hill—a rather gruesome murder. It involved Elsie Whipple, the ward of Philip Van Rensselaer and his wife's niece, and her lover, one Jesse Strang who had earlier feigned his own murder to escape from his family. Together, Elsie and Jesse bumped off Elsie's husband, John. Jesse swung for it, but Elsie got off scot-free thanks to her influential connections. Jesse's execution took place on the present location of the Mall and attracted more than 30,000 people who came from all over the county to watch him die.

Cherry Hill is located at 523½ South Pearl Street and is open Tuesday–Saturday 10–4, Sunday 1–4. Closed Easter, Thanksgiving and the day before, December 24, 25, 31 and January 1. Admission: Adults, $2; senior citizens, $1.50; children between 6 and 17, 75¢. Phone: 518-434-4791.

The Executive Mansion   This building, the original part of which was built by Thomas Olcott in the 1850's (see page 40), has many of the characteristics of the Queen Anne style—clustered chimneys, lots of turrets, gables and porches and a tower—but little of the beauty. Big and rambling, without much warmth, this place is enough of an atonement for any sins the governor may commit; after all, he's got to live there throughout his term. There is, however, a very decent art collection. The Man-

sion is at 138 Eagle Street, one block south of the Mall. Tours
are available Thursday only at 1, 2 and 3 P.M. Admission: Free.
Reservations required one week in advance. Phone: 518-474-2418.

Environs of Albany

Fort Crailo State Historic Site Just across the river in
Rensselaer, this manor house was begun about 1704, while the
rear wing was added in 1762. A house on this site was ordered
built by Kiliaen Van Rensselaer, the first patroon, in 1642, but
nothing of it remains. The present building was presented to the
state by the Van Rensselaer family in 1924.

Fort Crailo—the name in Dutch means "crow's woods"—still
has a feeling of Europe about it; leaded, diamond-paned windows, wood-paneled walls, heavy beams—and it has all been
restored to look like a house in the mid-seventeenth century but
is, I suspect, rather better furnished. Although a private house,
it was once used as a fort, and you can see loopholes for rifles
in the 21-inch-thick walls of the main building.

It was here in 1758, or so one story goes, that Dr. Richard
Shuckburgh, a British Army surgeon, composed the verses for
"Yankee Doodle" while sitting at the well in the garden. His
inspiration was the arrival of the New England troops in Albany to reinforce the British in their war against the French.

Open: April–December, Wednesday–Saturday 10–5, Sunday
1–5; January–March, Saturday and Sunday only, Saturday
10–5, Sunday 1–5. Admission: Free. Phone: 518-463-8738.

Rensselaerville and Other Things to
See and Do in Albany

About 27 miles southwest of Albany lies the absolutely charming and very small village of Rensselaerville, which was established in 1787. Drive out of Albany on Route 443 to Route 85,
which will take you right into the village. The road itself is
beautiful after you leave Albany, and as you travel south there
are some wonderful views of the Catskills looming ahead. The
village itself seems to have been plucked whole out of the eighteenth and early nineteenth centuries and is among the most

Tiny Rensselaerville, one of the most beautiful villages in New York State, is filled with houses that people dream of making their own.

delightful towns in the state. One of the primary reasons it has remained in such pristine condition is that a well-to-do local family bought and restored many of its houses and then resold them to visitors who couldn't resist their obvious charms. Today Rensselaerville is an oasis of peace, a wonderful place to take a stroll in and enjoy the perfectly cared for homes. My particular favorite is to the left as you enter the main street and down at the bottom of the hill. Known as the Conkling House and built in 1825, it's quite small with a low roof and windows in arched openings. But best of all is the minute portico with its three slender columns that give the whole a surprisingly elegant look.

You also should take time to walk on the blocks around the **Capitol** and **Mall**. Many of the buildings have been carefully restored, and there are some pleasant shops and interesting architecture. Be sure to take a look at the **Albany Academy** (1815) in Academy Park next to the Capitol. This was designed by Philip Hooker (1766–1836), the city's greatest native-born architect, and he may have been inspired by New York City's masterful City Hall. In any case, this is a very good-looking and elegantly classical building, one of the last survivors from its period in all of Albany.

Nearby, opposite the Capitol at the head of State Street, is Henry Hobson Richardson's **City Hall** (1882) and within the adjacent **Court of Appeals** is a splendid Court Room also designed by Richardson.

I would also suggest that you stop in to see the Gothic Revival **St. Peter's Church** designed by Richard Upjohn and constructed in 1859. Upjohn's most famous masterpiece is Trinity Church, built in 1846 in Gothic Revival style, in New York City. There are handsome stained-glass windows—the Burne-Jones window, second from the rear on the east aisle, was called by Matthew Arnold "the finest piece of stained glass in America" —and a particularly beautiful silver communion service donated by Queen Anne to the church in 1712. A second service, sent by the Queen at the same time, is still used by the Mohawk Indians in Canada.

At the foot of State Street is one of my favorite buildings, **State University Plaza**, built in 1918 by a local architect named Marcus T. Reynolds and modeled after the clothmaker's Guild Hall in Ypres, Belgium. It is a particularly striking building and has a six-foot weather vane representing Henry Hudson's ship, the *Half Moon*. Once the offices of the Delaware & Hudson Railroad, it was taken over in 1978 by the State University for its central administration offices.

Last of all is the **First Church in Albany**, on North Pearl Street at Clinton Avenue, which was organized in 1642 by a missionary from the Netherlands. The present church, built in 1799, was designed by Philip Hooker and can boast that both the oldest pulpit and the oldest weather vane in America belong to it.

COLUMBIA COUNTY

Hudson

Just after the Revolution, some of the most prominent whaling families in Nantucket somehow got convinced that Great Britain would never allow the permanent loss of her colonies. They knew that their island home, out there in the Atlantic, would be particularly vulnerable in any new war coming from England. So they decided to move to a safer place. Early in 1783, Seth and Tom Jenkins, two Nantucket brothers, carrying a sum of $100,000, set off to look at possible sites. They explored Long Island and even New York City, but eventually settled on a spot 100 miles up the Hudson, at a place called Claverack Landing, which was later renamed Hudson.

That fall, and throughout 1785, a number of families moved there not only from Nantucket but also from Martha's Vineyard, Providence and Newport. By 1784, they had established the present grid-pattern layout, and in 1785 the city of Hudson was incorporated.

Being pure-bred Yankees, they planned the whole operation down to the last wooden-peg nail. The families moved by sea, in their whaling ships, so that they could bring their household

Once famous for its whaling ships, then for its notorious red-light district, Hudson has since settled into a quiet river community offering a treasure trove of old houses to weekenders seeking secondary homes.

furnishings and supplies with them—indeed, many lived aboard their vessels until the new houses were completed—and would also have, ready-made, an impressive whaling fleet. By 1786 the town had grown fast enough to boast of 1,500 people, and its industries included a sperm oil works, a shipbuilder, a distillery, and various sail- and rope-making operations.

The whalers prospered until the embargoes prior to the War of 1812 came into effect, and then the war itself destroyed what remaining trade they had been able to maintain. It was not until 1830 that whaling was revived, and gradually the city began to thrive once more. In fact, other Hudson River towns —Poughkeepsie and Newburgh, in particular—began to compete for the rich profits, but none ever really rivaled Hudson. Soon Hudson was the commercial, political and industrial center of Columbia County, a position it still holds today. (Hudson became famous for something else; in the 1930's it had a notorious red-light district that gained it almost as much fame as its former whaling business. Gone forever, now, since the town decided to clean up its act, and weekenders have bought up and restored the old houses.)

Hudson is well worth a visit these days. Over the past few years the careful restoration of its fine old houses—many strongly influenced by the Nantucket whalers and looking slightly misplaced on the banks of the Hudson—has made the older sections of the city a treasure trove to wander through. By far the most interesting street is Warren Street, right in the heart of this little metropolis.

My particular favorite is the old **Bank of Hudson** (c. 1809) at 116 Warren. It was built by a man named John C. Hogeboom during the middle of a depression, hardly a good time you might think to start a bank—and you'd be right, for the bank soon failed. Hogeboom, ever resourceful, turned it into his private house. In the Federal style, the brick edifice has some Adam detailing that lends it a distinction that would make it notable anywhere. I'm thinking in particular of the four elegant white Ionic pilasters—note the tiny heads between the scrolls—that march across its façade and the two marble medallions decorated with swagged draperies between the windows of the first and second floors that give what is, after all, a rather small building a look of originality and elegance.

Across the street, at number 113, is the **Robert Jenkins House** (1811), now owned by the local branch of the Daughters of the American Revolution who have set it up as a museum of local history. Another Federal building, its interior was entirely —and mistakenly—reorganized in the early part of this century, but the façade retains that wonderful, soothing sense of classical proportion that is a joy to look at; I'm particularly fond of the steps and railing leading up to the handsome front door.

The third house of distinction is the **Cyrus Curtiss House** (c. 1834–37, with a wing added c. 1870) at 32 Warren, which would look totally at home on Nantucket. Curtiss was involved in whaling and also had a profitable oil and candle works that allowed him to build this imposing and substantial residence. Unfortunately, Curtiss' business burned to the ground—twice, in fact—and he was forced to sell his house to one Seneca Butts, a name I can't help but pass on. This Greek Revival house with an octagonal widow's walk is severe overall but made quite beautiful by its detailing: the elaborate grillwork at the attic level and above the front door, for example, not to mention the extremely well-done porch with its two Doric columns flanking

Incredibly, this building in Hudson was built as a bank—smack in the middle of a depression. Needless to say, it immediately failed and was converted into a private dwelling.

the door and two Ionic columns supporting the porch itself, all four painted stark white.

Other Things to See and Do

American Museum of Fire Fighting   The first few times I visited Hudson I skipped this museum thinking it would be boring. How wrong I was. It's fascinating and a wonderful place to visit. Ask any child. Located adjacent to the Firemen's Home —when you drive up you'll see the residents out enjoying the sun or strolling about—the museum boasts a collection of fire equipment and memorabilia dating back to 1725 that has to be among the most complete in the country. Wandering through it makes you feel like a kid again.

Far and away my favorite single thing in the collection is the **Statue of a Fire Chief**, originally from Coney Island of all places, and one of the best pieces of folk carving you'll ever see. Probably done about 1850, there he stands, or rather strides, his right arm flung out, huge silver trumpet to his lips, in his sky-blue coat lined with red. He's the epitome of gallantry and dash, everybody's image of the brave fireman to the rescue.

There are also some wonderful pictures to see—Currier and Ives prints, among others—and some absolutely incredible decorated fire engines from the nineteenth century. To mention only one, don't miss the **Hose Carriage, Weiner Hose Company No. 6** of Kingston, beautiful and fanciful enough to have taken Cinderella to the ball. It was never used to put out fires, only for parades, and consequently every attention was lavished to make it as stunning as possible. Item: The hose reel is encased in etched mirrors and is supported by silver-plated lions. Item: The crowning touch on the summit is a silver-plated fireman rescuing a child. Item: The wheels are an impossible 68-inches high. But then the whole museum is like that, full of surprises and treasures and fantasies, and you should allow yourself enough time to enjoy it.

Located on Harry Howard Avenue (he was one of New York City's greatest fireman heroes), the museum is open April–November, daily except Monday, 9–5. Admission: Contribution. Phone: 518-828-7695.

Environs of Hudson

Olana This, the most original—some would say bizarre—
house on the Hudson, was built by the painter Frederic Church
(1826–1900) in 1874. Although Calvert Vaux worked on it, Church
remarked, justifiably, that "as the good woman did about her
mock turtle soup, 'I made it out of me own head.'" Of the site
itself he wrote: "About one hour this side of Albany is the center
of the world—I own it." He exaggerated only a little. Perching
500 feet above the Hudson—Olana means "our castle on high"—
it offers one of the two or three most spectacular views of the
river and the Catskills, a view that Church was to paint many
times and in all seasons. Whether or not you tour the house,

*Olana, Frederic Church's bizarre creation, of which he said "as the good
woman did about her mock turtle soup, 'I made it out of me own head.'"*

you must see this spectacular panorama stretching for miles.

Church was not only the most famous landscape painter of his time but also the most successful. He studied with Thomas Cole, one of the leading lights of the Hudson River School, even living with him for a few years. Church then traveled extensively and became world-famous and rich from his exotic and huge South American landscapes, in particular "The Heart of the Andes" now in the Metropolitan Museum in New York City, as well as for such American-inspired paintings as "The Great Falls, Niagara," presently in Washington at the Corcoran Gallery. Church's canvas of "Icebergs," recently rediscovered in England, sold for $2.5 million in 1979, at the time the highest price ever paid for an American painting. These vast pictures, with their dazzling use of light and color, have the effect of putting the viewer right into the subject matter and are on such a grand scale that one's final feeling is that of awe, creating in some a near-mystical experience.

By the time Church built Olana he could afford to do exactly as he pleased, and what he pleased was to create a Moorish extravaganza of yellow stone, glazed Mexican and Persian tiles, polychrome brick, wooden decoration and, on the turret roof, colored slate. I don't think I like it, but I can't say I dislike it, either. I keep looking at it, trying to make up my mind. I guess overall I'm fond of it. It's so innocent, somehow, that it's hard to feel any animosity. It's a big, overgrown playhouse built by a child with an overworked imagination and too much money.

Inside, as far as I'm concerned, the paintings by Church (and a few others) are all that matter. Jammed to the rafters with furnishings, every inch of wall and floor crammed with some horror or other, the place is a Moorish-Victorian kitsch nightmare. But once again it's oddly fascinating as one man's peculiarly exotic vision.

Olana lies five miles south of the city of Hudson on Route 9G and is part of a 250-acre park that is open to the public for boating, picnicking and nature walks. The house itself is open late May–October, Wednesday–Saturday 9–5, Sunday 1–5. Admission: 50¢, children under 12 free. Phone: 518-828-0135. The grounds are open year-round from 8 until sunset—and if you can, try and see a sunset over the Hudson from here. What a sight!

Clermont The difference between Clermont and Olana is that between night and day. Where Olana's view is romantic drama, Clermont's is classically intimate, the Hudson almost at your feet. Olana is exploding exuberance, Clermont restrained elegance. Of the two, I prefer Clermont, both for the house, light and airy and definitely one in which you could happily settle, and for the grounds, which I love to wander through at all times of the day and in every season, to enjoy the banks of lilies, the beds of roses, the venerable old trees and lilac bushes, the vast undulating lawn, the hushed woods and, beyond it all, the omnipresent Hudson. The times I've been there I've had the place almost to myself and have enjoyed it most early in the morning when the light is crystalline, or at sunset which, from here, is poignantly intimate, as if it were a special display put on just for you.

This estate was founded by Robert Livingston (1654–1728), who was born in Scotland but spent a good part of his youth in Holland, which stood him in good stead when he came to America and then to Albany in 1673. He was successful almost from the beginning and soon allied himself to the patroon system (see

Clermont, white and classically elegant, has looked upon the Hudson for over 200 years, ever since the British burned the old structure and this was built on the same site.

page 25) through his marriage in 1679 to Alida Schuyler Van Rensselaer. In 1683 Livingston purchased 2,000 acres from the Indians, the foundation for an estate that would eventually encompass 160,000 acres—achieved, to put it gently, by hook or by crook. This became the Lordship and Manor of Livingston and secured his family's fortune. When he died he left the Manor to his eldest son, Philip, and the portion known as Clermont to Robert, Jr.

The family has since produced many distinguished men, but the most famous was Livingston's great-grandson, Robert R. (1746–1813), first Chancellor of New York State and the man who administered the first oath of office to George Washington in 1789. He also served in the Continental Congress, was involved in drawing up the Declaration of Independence, helped negotiate the Louisiana Purchase while minister to France under Thomas Jefferson and even introduced merino sheep into the country, thereby vastly aiding in the development of American woolen manufacture.

During the Revolution, in October 1777, Clermont was burned to the ground by the invading British, right after they destroyed Kingston (see page 86). Undaunted, the Livingstons rebuilt it, essentially in the same Georgian manner as the old house. Later, in the 1870's, a roof "in the French style" was added, giving the house the appearance you see today.

In 1803, when Livingston was in Paris, he met Robert Fulton and became his partner in building a workable steamboat, which first appeared on the Hudson in 1807, and became known as the *Clermont* after the Livingston estate. Fulton himself married Livingston's cousin, and the two men soon gained a monopoly on steamboating on the Hudson until it was declared unconstitutional in 1824 by Chief Justice John Marshall with Daniel Webster arguing for the antimonopolists.

The 450-acre **Clermont State Historic Park** is 16 miles south of Hudson off Route 9G—watch for signs—just on the border of Dutchess County. (For political reasons, the original Robert Livingston didn't want to have any land in Dutchess County.) The grounds are open all year from 8 until sunset and picnic facilities are available. The house itself is open only late May–October, Wednesday–Saturday 10–5, Sunday 1–5. Hours subject to change after Labor Day. Admission: Free. Phone: 518-537-4240.

A Drive through Columbia County

In many ways Columbia is the most beautiful county on the Hudson, both in the richness of its landscape and in the diversity and quality of its architecture. Back in the early 1800's Washington Irving depicted this region as consisting of "little retired Dutch valleys, found here and there embosomed in the great State of New York [where] population, manners, and custom remain fixed." His description still holds amazingly true, and the drive that follows should give you a taste of the best Columbia has to offer. You can do it in a few hours, but to fully enjoy it plan on a leisurely day.

Begin at Hudson, following Route 23B where it divides from 9G, following the sign for Claverack. As you approach this little village, the first county seat, be sure to note the houses, some of which go back to the eighteenth century and lend the village considerable charm. You soon will come to a crossroad; turn left

The 1767 Dutch Reformed Church in Claverack, perhaps the loveliest house of worship in Columbia County. This wing, added about 1850, is perfectly integrated into the older building, with its long green shutters running the length of both window and door.

and go north on 9H. Almost immediately, on your right, you will see a sign for the **Reformed Dutch Church**, the prettiest place of worship in the county. Turn into the drive and take a few minutes to enjoy this appealing building built in 1767. (The wings were added about 1850.) The brick has aged to a warm, rosy pink, and along the side facing the road the numerals of the year it was built have been laid into the brick above the windows. The windows themselves, beautifully proportioned, are set off by deep-green shutters that add a touch of elegance to the simplicity of the design. As you walk around the outside of the church, you will note that the wings have been perfectly integrated into the whole; for instance, at the center of each is a door surmounted by a window, and the shutters here run the length of both, balancing proportionately with the windows along the side. Inside, the pale-green walls and white ceiling are divided by a graceful balcony around the sides and back. The overall feeling is one of welcome, a place for families to gather, not a formal house of worship.

The church did have its problems, though. One of the more august Van Rensselaers was principally responsible for its being built and, staunch patroon that he was, he put in a pew for himself and his family that was not only elevated above all the other parishioners' seats but also had a canopy. This ostentation did not sit well with the rest of the congregation and eventually led to a schism. Here, too, the last minister in America required to preach in the Dutch language arrived—in the year of 1776, symbolically enough.

Continue north on 9H and within a few minutes, on your left, you'll see **Hotaling's Farm Market**, an irresistible roadside stand brimming with produce. The farm that supplies the stand, to give you an idea of its size, has 50 acres of sweet corn, 8 acres of pumpkins, grows annually 6,000 cabbages and 7,000 tomato plants, and features a pick-your-own orchard—apples, cherries, plums, apricots. They also make their own jams and jellies and fruit pies . . . but why go on? It's open every day from 9 to 5, a delight to the eye and palate, but fearsome on the pocketbook because you'll want to buy everything in sight.

Back on the road, you'll be driving through open, rolling farmland, and as you approach Kinderhook you'll see a sign for **Lindenwald** to your left. This was the home of Martin Van

Lindenwald, home of Martin Van Buren, eighth President of the United States and, later, home of Winston Churchill's grandfather, who won it gambling.

Buren (1782–1862), eighth president of the United States (1837–41). A Jacksonian Democrat, Van Buren is almost forgotten today (unfairly, most historians think) and failed twice (in 1840 and 1848) to get reelected. (He was so unpopular in Virginia in 1848 that he received only nine votes—which prompted one Virginian to remark, "We're still looking for that son-of-a-bitch who voted nine times.") It is thanks to him that "OK" entered the language; Van Buren used to call himself Old Kinderhook, and soon the initials took on a life of their own.

Van Buren bought Lindenwald in 1839. At the time it was a Federal-style mansion where Washington Irving had once frequently visited and was even for a short period tutor to the children of the house. (It was during this earlier time—the turn of the century—that Irving first became engrossed in the local legends and folk tales that would later appear in some of his most famous stories, in particular "The Legend of Sleepy Hollow." See the Van Alen House below.)

It was Van Buren's youngest son who decided that he wanted an Italianate villa and in 1848 hired Richard Upjohn, whose most famous achievement is Trinity Church (1846) in New York City, to remodel the house into a comfortable 36-room mansion with a four-story brick tower. It later passed out of the family —one of the owners was to be Leonard Jerome, Winston Churchill's grandfather, who won it, one story has it, while gambling with Van Buren's son—and was only taken over by the Federal Government in 1974, when it was established as a National Historic Site. (Currently being restored, the grounds are open to the public 9–5 every day but Thanksgiving, Christmas and New Year's Day. There are free conducted tours of the house daily, from June to mid-September. Phone: 518-758-9689.)

Just a little beyond this site, and again on your left, is the 1737 **Van Alen House**, in which the Van Alen family lived until 1964. The Columbia County Historical Society has since bought and restored the house as an example of Dutch life during the eighteenth century. It is extremely well done and shouldn't be missed.

You park by a little white frame building that was moved here and lays claim to being the schoolhouse where Ichabod Crane taught. (The Van Alen House itself, local legend says, was Irving's inspiration for the home of Katrina Van Tassel, "plump as a partridge; ripe and melting and rosy-cheeked as one of her father's peaches," who inadvertently caused Ichabod's downfall.) Once you've passed a small pond, the home of a few busybody ducks, you walk up a short hill to the red-brick, one-and-a-half-story house, a rare survivor of Dutch architecture with its steeply pitched roof, parapet gables and separate outside doors for each of the rooms. It looks like a direct descendant of some medieval house in Holland—which it basically is.

The three main interior rooms have been restored with particular care and taste, and each has an open fireplace, unique to the Dutch style, with wide chimneys starting at the ceiling level. Primitive in feel, with exposed posts and beams, there also is a Dutch sturdiness that gives the house an appealing solidity, and the handsome furnishings, Delft tiles and pictures are all

The Van Alen House. Here lived Katrina Van Tassel, "plump as a partridge," who would cause the downfall of poor, besotted Ichabod Crane.

from the Netherlands or the Hudson Valley. The place affords a unique glimpse of the daily life of the old Dutch settlers and, because there usually aren't too many visitors, you should have the house to yourself. (Open Memorial Day–Labor Day, Tuesday–Saturday 10:30–4:30, Sunday 1:30–4:30. It also is open weekends during September and October, same hours, as weather permits. Admission: $2. Phone: 518-758-9265.)

Now follow the signs into **Kinderhook**, and just as you approach the triangle where the road crosses Route 9, turn left into Apple Pie Square, a name too cute by half. If you're ready for lunch, eat here at The Treasure Shop, a very nice little restaurant surrounded by pleasant stores in the same building. The breads, soups and desserts are all homemade and delicious, and it makes for a nice break. It also is very reasonable. (Open Monday–Friday 9–6, Saturday 9–5, Sunday 1–5. No credit cards.)

Kinderhook, a lovely village, got its name from Henry Hudson when he anchored here in 1609. The ship quite naturally aroused the curiosity of the local Mohican Indian children, who came to gaze at this strange beast, and Hudson promptly named the spot Kinderhook, or Children's Corner. By 1640 the area had been settled, and today it is a virtually unspoiled setting for eighteenth- and nineteenth-century architecture good enough to merit its inclusion on the National Register of Historic Places.

To get a feeling of the village, walk south on Route 9, which here is called Broad Street, to the **House of History** (c. 1820). This exquisite example of Federal architecture, one of the most sophisticated of its type in the Valley according to some historians, was once the home of James Vanderpoel and is now owned by the Columbia County Historical Society. It is open to the public as a museum of the Federal period. One curious feature of the brick exterior is that front and back are identical, making the building not only completely symmetrical—four chimneys, four windows on two floors on each side of a central door with a fanlight and beautiful Palladian window—but "reversible." The real beauty of the exterior, though, comes from its completely realized sense of design and proportion. Once inside, the first thing you notice is the curved stairway, extremely sophisticated and graceful; the rooms, with their architectural detail and delicate ornamentation, are all lovely and furnished with some fine examples of the New York furniture of the period.

In the upstairs hall there is an added bonus, a small gallery of paintings including some that are choice. My particular favorite is a life-size portrait of Sherman Griswold and his wife Lydia by James E. Johnson (c. 1810–1858), a local artist about whose personal life little is known. Griswold was a local nabob, and there he and Lydia stand, in their best clothes, their farm in the background. Sherman is holding a round box from which a ram is feeding. Apparently it was the custom in the area for the men, after church each Sunday (which also explains the finery), to feed their sheep. Around this time, wool constituted an important industry in the county, partly due to the introduction of merino sheep by Robert Livingston at Clermont (see page 51). This portrait is particularly endearing; partly it's the gentle expression on the faces of the Griswolds, partly it's the way Lydia holds her husband's arm, and partly it's the sheep, one in particular who passively awaits her turn at the salt. Sad to note, Mr. Griswold eventually lost his money and his farm through railroad speculation, and even now it's hard not to feel a twinge of sympathy for such a kindly looking man. (The museum is open Memorial Day–Labor Day, Tuesday–Saturday 10:30–4:30, Sunday 1:30–4:30, also on weekends in September and October in good weather, same hours. Admission: $2. Phone: 518-758-9265.)

When you leave, walk a little further south where you will see the **David Van Schaack Mansion** (1774), which is identified by a historical marker. This private house, a magnificent specimen of Georgian architecture with eight wonderful chimneys and wings added during the early part of the nineteenth century, even has a small cemetery on its grounds where one past owner buried his slaves.

During the Revolution, General Burgoyne and his captors were entertained here by the Van Schaacks after "Gentleman Johnny's" defeat at Saratoga. The Van Schaacks, loyalists in sympathy to begin with, were not helped when one of their young children proposed a toast to England's royal family in front of Burgoyne's Yankee escort. (Kinderhook was more divided in its loyalties than most towns in the Hudson Valley, particularly among the conservative landowners.)

When you leave Kinderhook, after wandering along a few of its attractive streets, go back out on the same road you entered on until you see a sign for Chatham and Ghent where you will turn right. (This is Columbia County Route 21.) The winding country road will take you through scenery that approaches perfection, with distant views of the mountains to the east, and large cattle and horse farms on either side. Continue following the Chatham signs—this means a left at 21B, then turn right on 203, and left again (north) at 66, which should take you into **Chatham**.

Chatham was once a major railroad center, more than a hundred trains a day passing through, and the station, on your left as you enter the village, was built in 1887 to reflect this importance. It is now on the National Register of Historic Places, looking handsome but rather forlorn. In any case, as you pass the railroad station, turn left into the street that runs behind it and stop at the Depot Square Butcher Shop. They have something I'd never had before and haven't seen since, and you might like some, too. I'm talking about a horseradish-cheddar cheese so good you can't stop eating it. Unfortunately, everybody else likes it too; the last time I was there the butcher had run out of it. "I got twenty pounds yesterday and sold the last half-pound ten minutes ago," he told me.

If you're lucky enough to get the cheese, you can munch on it as you continue north on 66 toward **The Shaker Museum** in Old Chatham. The right turn for the museum is hard to see, but it's just before a steel bridge, and there is a sign for the museum here. This road will lead you through a countryside of elegant houses and horse farms with those wonderfully sinuous wooden fences that flow across the contours of the landscape. It is one of the prettiest areas of the county, proving that money well spent has nevered diminished Mother Nature's natural talents. Go past the sign for the museum's entrance to take a look at Old Chatham, about 1.5 miles farther. (It sometimes seems that there are an infinite number of Chathams in the county.) This little group of buildings is appealing, in particular one large old brick house with brick pillars. Then turn back and enter the dirt road that leads to the museum.

The Shakers have a long and honorable history, much of it in the Hudson Valley where their first community was established. The movement was founded across the Atlantic by Ann Lees (much later, in America, to be called Lee) who was born in Manchester, England, in 1736. In 1758 Ann Lees joined a small group of Quakers, but Quakers with a slight difference—they would sit in silent communion, like all Quakers, but at some point during their meditations they would be taken with "a mighty shaking."

In 1762 Ann married a blacksmith named Abraham Standerin (or Stanley—the name is spelled variously) and then, in quick succession over the next few years, lost four children in infancy. Bad enough in themselves, these deaths further traumatized Ann because each delivery had been extremely difficult. She came to see her tragedy as a judgment from God and began to avoid sexual relations with her husband. When she went to bed with him, she said, she felt "as if I had been in a bed of embers," hardly surprising in view of the results. Eventually this and other factors led to a conversion—"My soul broke forth to God," she later wrote—and she went out into the world with a tiny band of six or seven followers. Several times Ann and her group were arrested for disturbing the peace. (Understandable perhaps, since she preached that the two sexes living together was the source of all the evil in the world and that men and women must be treated as equals—but exist apart.) These ideas are still considered radical enough today, so it's no wonder Ann ended up in an English jail. There she had her single most important vision—Jesus came to her and became one with her. It was the second coming, but this time the spirit resided in a woman.

Once out of jail she became known as Mother Ann, or Ann the Word, and was soon having visions telling her to go to America. On May 10, 1774, Mother Ann and eight members of her band (including her husband, from whom she was already separated) sailed from England, bound for New York City, where they arrived on August 6. Upon disembarking, she marched her group up to a house where a family named Cunningham was sitting on their stoop, addressed them by name—she had no way of knowing it—and announced that they were to take her and her followers in. Astoundingly enough, they did.

This little band of Shakers soon heard of some land, available cheap, located about eight miles northwest of Albany, called by the Indian name of Niskayuna (now Watervliet), and there they settled. By 1780 they were making converts and, in the eyes of Revolutionary patriots, trouble. The latter believed the Shakers were in collusion with the British, and Ann and some of her followers were thrown into jails in Albany and Poughkeepsie. It did their cause more good than harm—Americans have always been notoriously sympathetic with the underdog—and they were quickly released.

By 1781, the Shakers were established enough to undertake a mission to New England, which would eventually have highly favorable results, spreading their religion even further.

Three years later, in 1784, Mother Ann died. Luckily for the Shaker society (some might term it Divine Providence), she was succeeded by several superb leaders who would spread the faith not only throughout New England but to Indiana, Ohio and Kentucky as well. So successful were they that the United Society of Believers in Christ's Second Appearing (as they now called themselves) codified their beliefs and way of life in 1821 into the Millennial Laws (revised in 1845).

This fascinating document established the colony in the Hudson Valley at New Lebanon, New York, as "the first and leading Ministry" headed, originally, by Brother Joseph Meacham and Mother Lucy Wright. (It was Meacham who formalized a dual order of male-female leadership, based on the perfect equality of the sexes, that would prevail for the entire history of the Shaker movement.) Also, the laws organized groups of believers into "families . . . in order to accommodate and provide for the different circumstances of individuals in temporal things, and . . . for the advancement of spiritual travel in the work of rejuvenation, and the universal good of all the members, composing such society." (New Lebanon, for instance, at its height would have eight "families," each containing, ideally, 50 members. Over the years, the Shakers would establish 19 such major communities, with anywhere from 2 to 8 families in each, as well as several minor ones.)

Over each family were Elders and Eldresses. Their primary responsibility, of course, was "to oversee the family under their care" in all spiritual matters. Next came Deacons and Deaconesses, who were in charge of the material welfare of the family, and finally the Trustees, who were "to perform all business transactions, either with the world, or with believers in other families or societies."

Every aspect of communal life was touched on in the Millennial Laws. For instance, "The gospel of Christ's Second Appearing strictly forbids all private union between the two sexes, in any case, place, or under any circumstances, in doors or out." Also: "No members except those in the Deacon's or Trustee's order, may go from home, even off the farm, without liberty from the Elders."

On education: "Girls' school should be kept in the summer and boys' school in the winter, and they should never be schooled together." (All the same, their system of education was so highly regarded that many non-Shaker parents in the region sent their children to these schools.) You may wonder how the Shakers got their children. They were placed there either by parents or by trustees of orphans, who thereby relinquished all rights to them, and lived under caretakers' supervision. At maturity they had the right to leave or stay, as they chose.

On personal property: "No private interest or property is, or can be allowed of, in families that have come into the covenant relation of a full dedication."

And so on, down through clothing (no special pockets), the ordering of each day, how to keep dooryards and farms as neat as a pin—there are even five prescriptions "concerning locks and keys."

If all this makes the Shakers seem unnecessarily grim, well, they weren't—nor were they perceived to be so by their neighbors. After initial persecutions, they slowly but surely advanced to a position of deep respect from their fellow citizens. It wasn't only their industriousness and the quality of their produce and manufactured goods and the wonder of their farms (although these were the most beautiful in the country, many agreed) that earned them this respect. It was equally their emphasis on hospitality and charity. "Do all your work as though you had a thousand years to live and as you would if you knew you must die tomorrow." In their hymn, "Simple Gifts," so well-known to most of us from Aaron Copland's adaptation of it for his *Appalachian Spring* ballet score, the Shaker way of life is perfectly summed up, I think:

> 'Tis the gift to be simple,
> 'Tis the gift to be free,
> 'Tis the gift to come down
> Where we ought to be,
> And when we find ourselves
> In the place just right,
> 'Twill be in the valley
> Of love and delight.
> When true simplicity is gain'd,
> To bow and to bend we shan't be asham'd
> To turn, turn will be our delight
> Till by turning, turning we come round right.

The Society reached its apogee of about 6,000 members in the years just before the Civil War—throughout their history the Shakers had a membership total of about 17,000—and then slowly went into a decline whose last glimmerings are still with us today. They have lasted longer and gained more fame than any other idealistic community this country has yet produced. In their own time they were famous for their seeds and herbs, farm produce and leather goods, clocks and furniture, agricultural machines and implements, so much so that the terms "Shaker" and "quality" became synonymous. They were ingenious both as improvisers and improvers. It is to them that we owe the flat broom (devised by Brother Theodore Bates in 1798), the first circular saw in America and the clothespin, among other homely inventions.

But today they are perhaps most famous for the incredible beauty with which they imbued everything they made, from the most common kitchen utensil to household furniture that appears unworldly in its purity. "This strange people have fertilized the rugged hills of New England by their systematic industry," Nathaniel Hawthorne wrote in his short story, "The Shaker Bridal." To say the least. It is a legacy of extraordinary beauty unique in our modern-day existence.

The Shaker Museum here in Old Chatham, one of the largest in the world dedicated to Shaker culture, is housed in a low-lying complex of barn-red buildings, and their contents are displayed to perfection. Again, because it's off the beaten trail, you can be fairly certain you'll have the buildings and grounds mostly to yourself.

Aside from the exhibits of furniture and tools, there is a blacksmith's shop, a gallery devoted to small crafts, textile and weaving shops, nine period rooms, and a schoolroom. The entire place is fascinating and deeply moving in its simplicity. For me, two objects in particular symbolize the whole. The first lies just beyond the entrance, a large circular wooden foundry pattern hung high against a stark white wall beside three steps leading up into another exhibit space. So simple and evocative of an inner stillness are those bent radiating spokes that one is oddly moved, reminded once again of the aesthetic perfection that resides in a circle. The second object is a high chair in the dining room on the first floor full of such chairs and rockers. Exquisitely conceived, its lines are so delicate and graceful that it seems to float in its space, timeless, weightless as a feather. Such love went into making this piece. When I first saw it, in a special exhibit on the second floor, there was above it a reproduction of a letter from a Shaker sister to a non-member of the sect written in the 1940's when that particular community was coming to an end. In it she said that they could not repair a certain chair since the sister who would normally do it could no longer use her hands, crippled now from many years of such work. The whole museum is like this: a nostalgic—even heartrending—glimpse of a pure and devoted people.

The museum also has a gift shop that offers superb herbs, still grown in the tiny Shaker community of Sabbathday Lake, Maine, kits for making Shaker furniture, a wide selection of books on the group and even records of their music. (Open May 1–October 31, 10–5. The library is open year-round by appoint-

Set amidst horse farms and undulating hills, the Shaker Museum is one of the more interesting regional museums in New York State.

ment. Admission: $3.50; senior citizens, $3 and students, $2.50; children, $1.50, under 6 free. Phone: 518-794-9100.)

When you leave, turn right and follow this back-country road to its end, and you'll be on 66 once more. Turn left here, in Malden Bridge, and almost immediately, on your left, you will see an antique shop in an old house right on the road. This is **Willard Vine Clerk, Antiques**, and is a real find for lovers of early American furniture, folk art, paintings and various Shaker crafts. Because of the quality offered, prices are accordingly high, but this is definitely worth a stop. There are no fixed hours, so I suggest that you call ahead to make an appointment if you are interested. The number is 518-766-2516. No credit cards accepted.

Not too far beyond, this time on your right, you will see a sign for the **Malden Bridge Arts Center**, a small, well-done shop with good-looking pottery made by its husband and wife owners, Barbara Harnack and Michael Lancaster, as well as paintings, dried flowers and a small but thoughtfully chosen selection of antique furnishings, all placed in gallery settings. (Open Friday–Sunday, 11–5, or by appointment. Phone: 518-766-3616. Credit cards accepted.) From here it is only a few minutes back to Chatham.

GREENE COUNTY

Located on the west bank of the Hudson opposite Columbia County, this small county has one site that it is imperative to see. I'm not exaggerating when I say that it offers a view the peer of any in the Northeast.

The Catskill Mountain House Site

There is a place in this Valley so lovely that it transcends mere description to become a symbol of the profoundest yearnings within the soul of the beholder. James Fenimore Cooper called it "the greatest wonder of all creation" and, in his novel *The Pioneers* (1823), had Natty Bumppo remark that from here he could survey "all creation," the Hudson "in sight for seventy miles under my feet, looking like a curled shaving, though it [is] only eight long miles to its banks." The English writer Harriet Martineau, notorious for her outspokenly pro-abolitionist work, *Society in America* (1837), wrote that it was "the noblest wonder of the Hudson Valley" and that from it she could see the Green Mountains of Vermont (true) and the Atlantic Ocean (false). The view for her, she implied, was so awe-inspiring as to give a new meaning to the Act of Creation. Thomas Cole, founding father of the Hudson River School who lived in nearby Catskill, observed that "all Nature here is new to art" and philosophized that this "grand diorama" was far too sublime for him to paint. A lesser-known visitor termed it "one of the most glorious prospects ever given by the Creator to man's imagination." Even Frances Trollope, Anthony's mother and author of a book deeply critical of just about everything that America represented, was forced to admit her delight in it. What they were all talking and writing about was the view from the then world-famous Catskill Mountain House, perhaps the most beloved hotel in nineteenth-century America.

It all began in 1823 when Erastus Beach, a stagecoach operator, built a small inn of a dozen rooms he called Pine Orchard on a rock ledge, the Wall of Manitou, 2,500 feet above the floor of the Hudson Valley. It commanded a view of a good 50 miles (*pace,* Natty Bumppo) up and down the Hudson. In 1845 Erastus' son Charles took over the hotel and would continue running it for the rest of the century. He also expanded it. In its final form it became a magnificent structure, Greek Revival in style, with 13 handsome white pillars, their Corinthian capitals brilliantly gilded, marching across a deep piazza framed by extensive wings on either side and providing 300 rooms for its distinguished guests. Everyone—and I mean everyone—stayed here. Consider this partial but representative list: Henry James, Jenny Lind, Winslow Homer, Oscar Wilde, Ulysses S. Grant, Alexander Graham Bell, Mark Twain, Thomas Cole and virtually every other artist of the Hudson River school (but not, thank God, all at the same time), Washington Irving and President Chester A. Arthur, whom I mention because his daughter was such a horrifying brat she gave "acute discomfort to other children."

The Mountain House was the first great mountain resort in

the United States but, far more important, it became a symbol
of the new nation's wealth and recently discovered cultural
ambitions. The epitome of American aspirations in the nineteenth century, it was even credited by some as providing the
singular atmosphere necessary for the foundation of the American romantic movement. Who knows? Perhaps it did. It's certainly true that it exercised an authority over its visitors that
no hotel before or since in this country has ever done.

The Mountain House lasted well into the twentieth century,
falling into a slow decline that paralleled the rising national
boredom with all things romantic. Finally, in 1942, the last
guest left. By 1963 the state had taken it over, including its 3,000
acres of land, and because the by-now ramshackle building was
deemed dangerous, they burned it to the ground on January 25,
1963, at six in the morning. Gone forever was that "drift of snow
that had not melted in the spring," as one traveler described
seeing it from the valley.

Well, knowing all that, how could I not go and see the site for
myself? But, with one thing or another, I didn't. Not for years.
Perhaps it was because I was afraid nothing could live up to that
kind of advance billing. Or maybe it was plain old inertia. Finally I decided it was time—but how, exactly, did one get there?
All I knew was that it was near the town of Catskill. After
several phone calls I did get a route: Exit from the New York
State Thruway at Saugerties and then get on Route 32 to Palenville. Once there, follow 23A to Haines Falls, and then take a
right turn on County Route 18, where there is a sign for North
Lake State Campsite, and at North Lake they will give you a
map to the Mountain House site.

The drive turned out to be a beautiful surprise, for a good part
of it is through the Catskill State Park region. Once in the park,
you can immediately understand why painters have loved it so;
at the same time, you get the eerie impression that you are
moving through some kind of time-space continuum, for the
feeling is entirely of another era. Completely unspoiled, with
rushing streams, a ravishing waterfall, steep mountain slopes
and dark precipitous drops at the road's edge, this is certainly
"the forest primeval."

From the entrance booth to North Lake the drive grows more
prosaic, pretty woods with carefully marked trails, all rather

uneventful. North Lake, a small, sky-blue mountain tarn fringed with wooded slopes, has a parking lot and beach, and from there it's a short walk to the Mountain House site, upon which now rests merely a commemorative marker. As you approach the escarpment you still have no idea of what this view will be really like until, all of a sudden . . . Incredible! . . . There it is—the world at your feet! No other place in the Northeast has this kind of infinite glory, and while there are sites in other areas of the nation that are as splendid—the Grand Canyon, for one—none is more moving. It has to be one of the great natural sights in this world.

Straight ahead, you look west to the Taconic and Berkshire ranges, the Hudson a silky blue ribbon laid down the Valley. Clouds cast their plump shadows over the landscape, and here and there tiny little buildings add thumbprints of color to a landscape of greens and blues and browns and dove-gray. (I've read accounts of guests at the hotel watching thunderstorms in the Valley while bathed, themselves, in brightest sunshine.) Over all reigns a deep peace and quiet. It is no wonder that so many people have invoked the Creator while gazing out upon this view, for it awakens intimations not only of immortality but of omnipotence. To be more prosaic, it's like having in front of you a stupendous HO scale model of a good section of the earth, and you almost believe you can reach out and pluck up that red barn eight miles or so away and make it more effective by moving it, say, five miles farther north. As it happens, I have a terrible fear of heights, yet here I wasn't affected in the slightest by my phobia. Perhaps because I was so high in such a vast panorama that fear could no longer comprehend it. I stayed for more than half an hour, moving back and forth along the escarpment to enjoy the different vistas and to watch the changes in the shifting light patterns. Then I began to note the reactions of other visitors. Almost everyone did the same thing: As they approached they'd be chatting and then, when the full force of the prospect before them hit, they'd fall silent, even drift apart, and just look. It was a rare and thrilling experience, now a memory I shall always keep with me. I'm not even sure I'll go back. Could it ever be quite the same as that first time?

On leaving, I turned left at the first road beyond the entrance booth and followed the road to its end. Then I walked down a narrow dirt path and came out at the head of the **Kaaterskill Falls,** another great favorite of the romantics—Washington Irving called them "wild, lovely and shagged"—whose glories have been depicted by several of the more famous members of the Hudson River School, my particular favorite being an introspective study by Asher B. Durand now in the collection of The New-York Historical Society in New York City. Unfortunately, I couldn't see much. Given what I've already told you, to say that the drop down is longer than Niagara's explains why I didn't go anywhere near the edge. Next time I'll find out how —and if—one can approach it from the bottom. And anyway, in life there should always be one more thing to look forward to …or so I keep telling myself.

What to See in the Environs

The Bronck House Museum   In 1663 Pieter Bronck became the first builder on this land. (His father, Jonas, had a 500-acre "bouwerie" in New York City that later became the Bronx.) Today there stands on Pieter's property a little complex of buildings dating from 1663, 1685 and 1738 as well as various barns—Dutch, Victorian, and a famous one that's thirteen-sided.

It's a nice find and well worth your while if you're nearby. In the museum proper, there are paintings by Thomas Cole, John Frederick Kensett, Ammi Phillips and "the Schuyler limner" (see page 36), among others. There also are some excellent pieces of furniture and good examples of china and glass. In the barns are preserved fascinating local memorabilia, including a few of the famous capitals and other artifacts recovered from the Catskill Mountain House. All in all, a kind of grandmother's attic treasure trove of history—you'll enjoy your visit here, I promise.

The museum is about 4 miles south of Coxsackie, just off Route 9W on Pieter Bronck Road. Watch carefully—the sign for it is small and easily missed. Open: Last Sunday in June through last Sunday before Labor Day. Tuesday–Saturday, 10–5, but closed noon to 1 P.M. Sunday, 2–6. Admission: Adults, $1.75; children 12–15, $1.00, and 5–11, 50¢. Phone: 518-731-8386.

Where to Stay and Eat

Saratoga Springs
Area Code: 518

Where to Stay

The Gideon Putnam, Box 476, Saratoga Springs 12866. Phone: 584-3000. Rates: During July and August a single is about $135 per day, a double $200; add $50 for each additional person. Rates are lower for the rest of the year. Credit cards accepted.

This attractive colonial building, set right in the heart of the Saratoga Spa State Park grounds, is the best place to stay in Saratoga, and all facilities of the park, as well as all events at the Saratoga Performing Arts Center, are within walking distance. The rooms are comfortable, the service efficient, the food banal.

The Adelphi, 365 Broadway, Saratoga Springs 12866. Phone: 587-4688. Rates: During July and August a single runs to about $55, a double from $65 except on weekends and during the racing season when the rates shoot up to about $100 for a single and start from $120 for a double. Rates vary for the rest of the year. Credit cards accepted.

Built in 1877, this is the last whisper of Saratoga's great resort hotel days with its handsome, columned piazza and Victorian gingerbread decoration. Recently restored with turn-of-the-century furnishings and ornamentation, it attracts a younger crowd than the Gideon Putnam. The food, however, is on the same level.

Where to Eat (in order of preference)

Chez Sophie, 69 Caroline St. Phone: 587-0440. Credit cards accepted.

Far and away the best restaurant in Saratoga Springs in a house that boasts a small, pretty bar and several attractive dining rooms. Sophie, a French woman from Normandy, is the chef, and she and husband Joseph run the place with friendly, impeccable service. The menu is small and everything is cooked with consummate care. Very good indeed. Open: May–October. No lunch. Dinner: 6–9:30, during July and August in two sittings. Closed Sunday, July and August. Closed Sunday and Monday, June, September and October. Prix-fixe dinner, about $30. Reservations required.

Dacha,   Fiddler's Elbow Road, Middle Falls. Phone: 692-2188. Credit cards accepted.

This wonderful country restaurant, in quality on a par with Chez Sophie and a half-hour's drive out of Saratoga, is a great favorite and offers a menu that changes according to what's available in the markets and from the proprietors' own garden. Whatever is on the menu, though, rest assured that it will be first rate. Highly recommended. Open July and August. Pretheater dinner: 5:30. Dinner: 6–11. Open five days a week, but the days can vary. Call to check. Both prix-fixe (about $37) and à la carte offered. Reservations essential.

Mrs. London's Bake Shop,   33 Phila Street. Phone: 584-6633. Credit cards accepted.

Craig Claiborne, author and food critic for the *New York Times,* has favorably compared the pastries and breads here to the very best in Europe. Owners Michael and Wendy London and their staff bake everything you can think of, and to perfection: sticky buns that are out of this world, the best sourdough bread in the east, melt-in-your-mouth croissants, beautiful cakes and tarts and cookies, and on and on. Breakfast here at least once is a must, and they also offer a delicious light lunch selection, soup, quiche, sandwiches, salad, and so forth. Prices are high, but considering the quality every cent is well spent. Open seven days a week. Breakfast: 8–11:30. Lunch: 11:30–3.

The Union Coach House,   139 Union Avenue. Phone: 584-6440. Credit cards accepted.

Built in the 1870's, this restaurant is now a great favorite during the racing season, particularly since one of its owners is the daughter of one of the more famous racing families. It can be fun, it can be chic, but it's not a memorable place to eat, although reasonably priced. Steaks, chops, fish and pasta are the basic fare. Open: Tuesday–Saturday. Lunch: 11–12:30. Dinner: 5:30–10:30, to 12 midnight during the season. Sunday brunch in July and August: 11:30. Closed Sunday for dinner. Reservations suggested.

The Olde Bryan Inn, 123 Maple Avenue. Phone: 587-2990 or 587-9741. Credit cards accepted.

This 1773 building is pretty and inviting on the outside, cozy inside. It's a good bet for a reasonable lunch or dinner with nice sandwiches and burgers as well as more hearty entrées. Open daily 11:30A.M.–midnight.

Albany
Area Code: 518

Where to Stay

The Albany Hilton, State and Lodge streets, Albany 12210. Phone: 462-6611. Rates: For a single, from about $60; for a double, from about $75. Credit cards accepted.

For many years downtown Albany had no decent hotel. Fortunately, that has now changed and this Hilton is ideally located. Higher floors, with comfortable rooms, have a view of the Hudson or a splendid one of the Capitol and Mall. I always ask for the latter. The restaurants can easily be skipped; food and service range from poor to awful in settings that are tacky.

Where to Eat (in order of preference)

L'Hostellerie Bressane, Box 387, Hillsdale 12529. Phone: 325-3412. No credit cards accepted. About a 45-minute drive from Albany. (See page 75.)

Jack's Oyster House, 42 State Street. Phone: 465-8854. Credit cards accepted.

My favorite restaurant in Albany, this is right out of the late nineteenth century with wonderful old photos, no frills but inviting decor, excellent service and a large, no-nonsense menu that features, in particular, the biggest and best selection of seafood for miles around as well as steaks and chops. Because it's so good it's always crowded, and you must reserve for lunch and should for dinner. This is the one restaurant in town that's worth the trip and, to top it off, it's moderately priced, too. Daily specials run about $10. Open daily, 10:30 A.M. to 11 P.M.

L'Auberge, 351 Broadway. Phone: 465-1111. Credit cards accepted.

This restaurant is in a wonderful-looking old building that formerly housed the ticket office of the Hudson River Day Line. The inside, however, is a bit on the bleak side, but fortunately the menu offers very good French selections; I particularly remember an excellent lobster dish, the meat picked from the shell and served with pea pods in a delicate sherry-cream sauce and upon a bed of rice. Rather expensive, but generally worth it. Open daily. Lunch: 12–2:30. Dinner: 6–10. Closed Sunday and Saturday for lunch. Reservations suggested.

None of the remaining restaurants in Albany are all that special. However, if you like rubbing shoulders with politicians, you might try **Lombardo's,** 121 Madison Avenue. (Phone: 462-9180. Credit cards accepted. Reservations usually unnecessary.) Friendly old-fashioned waitresses—"What'll yours be, dear?"—wonderful murals, reasonable prices and huge portions help make up for the lackluster food. Open Wednesday–Sunday, 11:30–9.

There's also **Bella Napoli,** 97 Beaver Street. (Phone: 463-9771. No credit cards accepted. Lunch: 11:30–2. Dinner: 5–10:30. Closed Saturday. Reservations suggested.) More expensive, less décor, but better food.

The only other French restaurant of any note is **La Serre,** 14 Green Street. (Phone: 463-6056. Credit cards accepted. Lunch: Monday–Friday, 11:30–2:30. Dinner: 6–10, 10:30 Saturday. Closed Saturday for lunch and all day Sunday. Reservations suggested.) It's pretty, but the food is soon forgotten. Still, it seems popular, so perhaps I'm missing something.

For a hamburger or a snack, I can recommend the **Hudson River Trading Company,** 388 Broadway. (Phone: 465-8782. Credit cards accepted. Lunch: 11 on. Dinner: 5–11, to 1 A.M. on weekends. Closed Sunday. Reservations unnecessary.)

Columbia County
Area code: 518

Where to Stay

It's sad but true that there really is no great inn or hotel in Columbia County. I can make only three suggestions, and therefore I would also recommend that you consider **The Beekman Arms** (see page 128), within a comfortable driving distance of about thirty minutes from Hudson. Here, in order of preference, are my three recommendations.

Swiss Hutte, Hillsdale 12529. Phone: 325-3333. Rates: About $50 per person. Closed from November 1 to December 15. Credit cards accepted.

The best of the three in terms of general comfort and overall appeal, this inn sits practically on top of the Massachusetts border in the middle of the Clermont ski area. It offers a few rooms in the main inn, a cottage and motel-style rooms. The food here is good (see page 76) and there's a swimming pool.

The Inn at Shaker Mill Farm, Canaan 12029. Phone: 794-9345. Rates: About $35 per person, including breakfast. Open all year, reserve well in advance. No credit cards.

This small inn (15 rooms), not far from the Massachusetts border, is, indeed, a converted Shaker mill. Simply decorated, informally run, it may be a bit too Spartan for some. Yet guests here tend to mingle and many return, so it obviously has a dedicated following. On the plus side: Nearby cross-country skiing, a pond and pleasant walks in summer. On the (possibly) debit side: You'd better be friendly and love the communal approach to life . . . and be prepared to see a lot of New Yorkers.

L'Hostellerie Bressane, Box 387, Hillsdale 12529. Phone: 325-3412. Rates: about $55–$65. Closed during February and March or sometimes March and April, so please check. No credit cards accepted.

The food here is superb (see below), but the rooms—there are only a few, but they do have fireplaces—are simple and only two have private baths. Well, you can't have everything. Some solve the problem by eating a long, wonderful dinner and then staying overnight only.

Where to Eat

If I wanted to open a restaurant and was looking for a spot that was both beautiful and had very little competition, I'd settle for Columbia County. True, there is one near-great restaurant, but after that you're on your own and should consider using the restaurants in Dutchess County (see page 138).

L'Hostellerie Bressane,   Box 387, Hillsdale 12529. Phone: 325-3412. No credit cards.

This is the best restaurant in the Upper Hudson and could hold its own anywhere. The food is marvelous. The dining rooms, in an attractive old house, are comfortable and intimate with fresh flowers on all the tables. I especially remember one night when I had a combination of chicken and baby lobster in the most delicate sauce imaginable served with delicious vegetables, all beautifully presented on oversized plates. The balance of tastes was exquisite and what, in other hands, might have been on the bland side was, thanks to the art of Chef Jean Morel, a very special experience. For dessert, I bypassed one of his spectacular soufflés for oeufs à la neige, which were quite simply the best I've ever had. And then on to their excellent coffee and a selection from their wonderful cellar of cognacs, Armagnacs and Calvados. The menu changes according to what is available but I can honestly say that I've never had a meal here that hasn't met the highest standards. On the expensive side, yet worth every penny. But be sure to make reservations. Dinner only. As hours may vary, call to check. Closed Monday and Tuesday, except in July and August. Closed all of February and March, or March and April (it all depends—so check first).

The Swiss Hutte,   Hillsdale 12529. Phone: 325-3333. Credit cards accepted.

The "other" restaurant in Columbia County. This, too, is fairly expensive but not of the same quality. That's not to say the food isn't good, for it is, but it's just not worth a detour. The bar is particularly nice in winter, though, with a fireplace and good service at the tables. The menu is primarily French with a few other continental dishes thrown in.

THE
MIDDLE HUDSON
Ulster and Dutchess
Counties

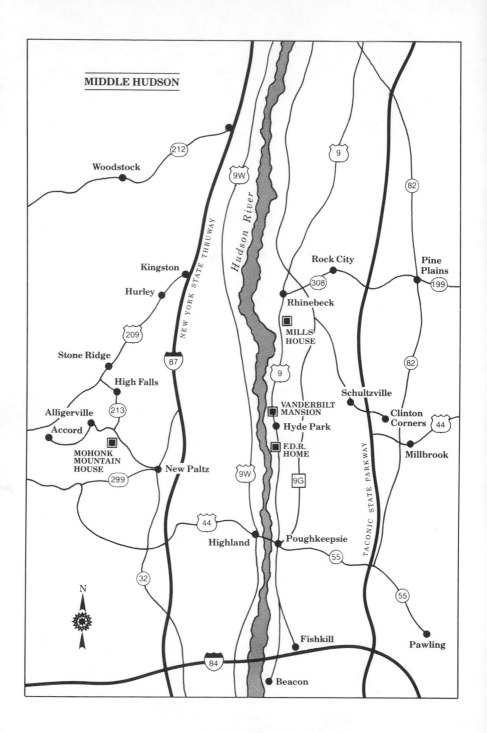

MIDDLE HUDSON

Woodstock

212

9W

9

Hudson River

NEW YORK STATE THRUWAY

Kingston

Hurley

Rock City

308

Rhinebeck

MILLS
HOUSE

209

Stone Ridge

87

High Falls

9

213

Schultzville

Alligerville

VANDERBILT
MANSION

Accord

Hyde Park

Clinton
Corners

44

MOHONK
MOUNTAIN
HOUSE

F.D.R.
HOME

Millbrook

299

New Paltz

9W

9G

TACONIC STATE PARKWAY

44

Highland

Poughkeepsie

32

55

55

N

Fishkill

Pawling

84

Beacon

THE swans are back. For the first time in years. And they've chosen this, the soul of the Valley, as the spot in which to build their nest, right in the dark green vegetation where Rondout Creek at Kingston joins the Hudson. To me it's exactly right that they should be here, dead center in the most beautiful and tranquil section of the River, where it flows through Dutchess and Ulster counties.

No other place in America is quite like the Middle Hudson. As in certain parts of Europe, past, present and future merge here in a seamless flow; a spirit of equality rather than of struggle. It gives the area a timeless stability that lifts you out of yourself; you've finally and truly gotten away from it all.

At the same time, this region is extraordinarily rich in its diversity: Ancient (by American standards) families struggling in genteel poverty to preserve a heritage handed down for more than three hundred years while living cheek by jowl with IBM, the company of the twenty-first century and the major employer in the area . . . River views unchanged and unchanging since Henry Hudson first arrived . . . The decayed old port of Rondout, its ugly contemporary bridge swooping over—but not quite able to hide—the exciting renovation and revitalization slowly but steadily under way . . . Exquisite country roads, twisting and turning through woods and mountains, past wineries and thoroughbred horse farms, orchards and fields filled with corn.

Then there is the faintly pot-scented aroma of Woodstock (especially on Saturday nights), the all-American moneyed village perfection of Rhinebeck, the beautiful, lived-in restoration of old Kingston, the elephantine estates, the simple, unique-to-the-Hudson Dutch stone houses. Not to mention a vast nineteenth-century resort (Mohonk Mountain House), tiny bed & breakfast hostelries, the oldest inn in America in continuous operation (The Beekman Arms) and, among many excellent restaurants, the greatest in the Valley and a superb eating place by any standards (the DePuy Canal House). And over all there is the light—that light so beloved by the Hudson River artists who lived and worked here, a light that gives the green of the Valley its special depth and richness and clarity. The time you spend here will be richly rewarded.

ULSTER COUNTY

Kingston

Kingston is one of the undiscovered treasures of the Hudson. A small city of about 25,000 people that lies 90 miles north of New York City, it retains, perhaps more than any other town on the Hudson, its centuries-old, balanced relationship with the river. Possessing that increasingly rare quality of honest charm, it's nevertheless sophisticated enough to support a four-star restaurant (within 20 minutes' driving distance) and offers a boat ride through scenery that can only be described as achingly beautiful. There's also an antique shop of museum quality, more than 20 of those handsome seventeenth- and eighteenth-century Dutch stone houses, and a church that Calvert Vaux, co-designer of Central Park in New York City, described as "ideally perfect."

HISTORY

Kingston was first settled in 1652 by the Dutch, who called it Wiltwyck, a name that stuck until the English took over. As the settlers began moving out into the surrounding areas the local Esopus Indians, members of the Algonquin tribe, grew restless enough to go on the warpath. They were promptly crushed, but Peter Stuyvesant, Dutch governor of New York from 1647 until 1664, when the English ousted him, was upset enough to order a simple stockade built in 1658 that would surround the settlement and protect the area. A good thing he did, too; the Indians attacked twice more, first in 1660 and then in June 1663, when they massacred a few settlers and burned everything in sight. (Why, by the way, are the Indians always referred to as "massacring" while the whites are only "defending" themselves as

Along the main street of Old Kingston the covering gallerias offer a fanciful touch that makes it a most attractive place down which to stroll.

they walk off with all the real estate?) This did not amuse Stuyvesant, who got on his silver-encrusted wooden leg and undertook a full-scale summer campaign that proved so successful the Indians' sway in the Valley was broken forever.

What to See and Do: A Perfect Day with Two Endings

Today what is called the Stockade District forms the oldest and most interesting section of the town, an area of several blocks that was once the heart of old Kingston. It is where I always head, first thing in the morning, whenever I visit Kingston, driving past the **Old Dutch Church** at the corner of Main and Wall streets and, a few buildings further on, just by the County Court House, leaving my car in the very convenient municipal parking lot. It's a short walk back to the church.

The original church on this site was built in 1661, but the present bluestone Renaissance Revival building dates from 1852, based on designs by Minard Lafever. (One of the most sought-after architects of the period, Lafever (1797–1854) was most famous for his Gothic Revival churches, but he also de-

signed other kinds of buildings and in other styles. Aside from
this church his finest works, I feel, are St. Anne's (1847) in
Brooklyn Heights in Gothic Revival style and the glorious
Greek Revival central building of Sailors' Snug Harbor, built in
1831, on Staten Island.) The Old Dutch Church here in Kingston
is a masterpiece. As Vaux said, "I cannot change a thing without impairing the exquisite unity."

To me the most perfect part of the church is its steeple, so
ideally proportioned that it seems weightless, ready to float
gently but purposefully upward, taking your heart right along
with it. Then you look down once again at the church itself, and
realize how comfortably it's situated, like the solid Dutch citizens it represents.

Given such a pretty spot, people are always about, sitting or
strolling in the tree-filled churchyard, watching the birds and
listening for the bells, and it's quite pleasant to wander a few
minutes here, reading the old gravestones that date back to 1710
and enjoying the different perspectives the building offers. If
you're lucky, you'll hear the bells play—"Onward, Christian
Soldiers" is what I usually get.

Inside, the building seems so totally without pretension that
it takes a moment to realize just how good is the whole, both as
a structure and in what it represents. It's the cumulative effect:
the handsome Tiffany window (1891) behind the pulpit; a framed
letter from George Washington to "the Minister, elders and
deacons" in which his fervent prayer is "that you may be ena-
bled to hand down your Religion pure and undefiled to a Poster-
ity worthy of their ancestors"; the elegantly vaulted ceiling, the
commemorative plaques throughout, the faded Civil War flags.

Leave the church through the office to the left at the back and
you're out again on Wall Street with enough time before lunch
for a short stroll. Turn right and, after a block or so, both sides
of the street become arcades covered by one-story white wooden
galleries topped with balconies. The buildings themselves,
mostly nineteenth century, are painted in complementary pas-
tels and along the sidewalks are well-spaced trees and judi-
ciously placed tubs of flowers. For some, the effect may smack
too much of a stage set—but it's not; it's an inviting, very pretty,
unified setting.

The shops—pharmacies, the Wellspring Bookstore with an

excellent section on the Hudson and local history, a friendly
little department store—are the usual things you'd expect to
find in a major town, but here there's still an aura of nineteenth
century friendliness and relaxation.

Cross over at the end of the street, go back up and turn right
on John Street. About halfway down and you're at **Schneller's**,
whose motto is "The wurst place in town" (see page 135). For
lunch, you certainly could do wurst. (Once started it's hard to
stop.) This unpretentious German restaurant has two entrances, with a store in between, but more about that later. Go
to the far entrance, which will lead you up a flight of stairs to
a cheerful Victorian room with high, arched windows where
you should have an absolutely delicious lunch.

All the sausages and breads and desserts are homemade, the
list of domestic and imported beers can't be faulted, the meats
are of prime quality, the unusual sandwich combinations are
terrific (Brie melted over bacon and tomato springs to mind), the
cheeseboard—with the cheeses at the exactly right stage of
ripeness—comes with an assortment of homemade breads,
the blueberry pancakes float right off the plate, the Linzer
torte brings tears to the eyes. Even the lemonade is perfection.

Stagger back down the stairs, and take a look at Schneller's
market, a find in a city of any size, with its farm-fresh butter,
pork chops smoked right there in back, a wonderful variety of
other meats and cheeses, not to mention a ridiculous gift shop
stuck off in a corner that is straight out of corniest Bavaria.
Next door is another excellent market with the best local produce, and between the two, you could create a terrific picnic
hamper.

By now you need a good walk, and what I usually do is continue down the street, then wander off through the **Stockade
District**, exploring any street that looks interesting (almost all
are). Study some of the stone houses. The nice thing is that
they're still used, some as private residences, others as offices,
and so they don't have that glazed restored-to-perfection look.
This is a town, remember, not a museum, with pleasant gardens
and yards to delight in, half-open Dutch doors to peek through,
historical plaques to read and, every now and then, a friendly
dog with a perpetual-motion tail, trying to cadge a pat or two.

Once you feel you've seen enough, turn back toward Wall Street, go again to the end, turn right and walk up to Clinton Street. You're now at the **Senate House** and its neighboring **Museum**. For information on current hours, programs, and exhibits, phone 914-338-2786.

I suggest you visit the museum first. It houses an extensive collection of paintings by John Vanderlyn (1775–1852), a Kingston native who is recognized primarily as one of the first native American landscape artists, but who was also a portraitist of some distinction. According to John Howat's *The Hudson River and Its Painters,* "Vanderlyn's ambition was to be a great painter of history in the tradition of Jacques-Louis David." Howat also quotes from a letter of introduction Vanderlyn's patron, Aaron Burr, wrote in 1801 in which he states that Vanderlyn "is pronounced to be the first painter that now is or ever has been in America."

Built in 1676, the Senate House now looks so ancient it seems to have sprung from the earth like the flowers in its hedged garden.

Indeed, Vanderlyn's paintings *are* good, particularly his portraits. True, there is a certain stiffness in some of the latter, despite his six years of study in Paris, but there are some very nice touches, too. A gently mysterious portrait of a young girl (Mrs. John R. Livingston) turned away from a mirror, yet with her profile reflected back to the viewer, is quite haunting. He's a nice "find" and the collection on display is large enough for you to get a thorough appreciation of his work. (By the way, the Metropolitan Museum in New York City now has on permanent display in its American wing Vanderlyn's enormous panoramic view of the gardens at Versailles.)

It's also interesting to know that Vanderlyn's grandfather Pieter (see page 37), who lived in Kingston part of his life, was one of the great folk artists of his time and a member of the first cohesive group of American portraitists, all of whom were centered in the Hudson Valley.

Upstairs, the museum displays temporary shows and a few things from its own collection. (My favorites: the steering wheel of the *Mary Powell*, "Queen of the Hudson," the most famous steamboat—aside from Fulton's—ever to travel the Hudson, and whose home port was Kingston, and a wonderful painting of the *City of Kingston* steamer by James Bard, a renowned "portraitist" of Hudson River vessels.) The small shows are usually quite imaginatively presented. One that I particularly remember was devoted to Ammi Phillips (1788–1865), who lived and worked in the Valley for many years and is considered one of the finest folk artists of the nineteenth century. This exhibit was introduced by a marvelous quote made in 1829 by John Neal, a long-forgotten American author (*Keep Cool* is one of his titles), that aptly sums up a more jaundiced approach to American folk art: "You could hardly open the door of a best-room anywhere without surprising, or being surprised by, the picture of somebody, plastered to the wall and staring at you with both eyes."

The Senate House, which you should visit next, is a small gem. Here you will see the kitchen, bedroom and parlor where the first official New York State Senate met. Actually, the house was the private residence of the Van Gaasbeek family, but when Kingston became the first capital of New York as the legislators fled here to escape the British, the Van Gaasbeeks let their home be used by the Senate. On April 20, 1777, the lawmakers adopted the state's first constitution, and George Clinton was chosen as governor two months later. While this building was being used by the Senate, the state assembly met in a nearby tavern, and Ulster County Courthouse served as both the capitol and the home of the Supreme Court. By October 1777, however, the British threatened again, and the government took off for Poughkeepsie just before the redcoats, under Major General John Vaughan, burned Kingston to the ground. Vaughan later explained his action by writing that the city was a "nursery for almost every villain in the country," a wild exaggeration since the legislators had left, and that upon "[our] entering the town they fired from their houses, which induced me to reduce the place to ashes, not leaving a house." Well, he was almost right. In fact, several buildings—including the one you're now visiting—survived.

Now, one more stop in the Stockade District. Go back to Wall Street and, opposite the church, knock at the door of **Fred J. Johnston, Antiques** (closed January–April) at the corner of Wall and Main. If you're serious about antiques, you cannot afford to miss this shop. It's "by appointment only" (phone: 914-331-3979) and expensive—much of the collection is of museum quality—and includes the most extensive and beautiful collection of Americana in the Valley.

Johnston specializes in superb examples of American furniture from all periods but particularly of the seventeenth and eighteenth centuries. He also has a vast store of paintings and prints, porcelains, watercolors, fraktur, glass, pottery . . . in essence, a cornucopia of early America that is the result of years of study and an innate feel for excellence. The shop is in a handsome two-story building set off to the side and back from the Federal house where you entered, with a handsome eagle from a Hudson River steamboat over the entrance. The interior is essentially two huge rooms, upstairs and downstairs, but so chock-a-block full, and so cleverly arranged, that you feel as if you're strolling through many different rooms.

Fred Johnston himself is a fascinating man with an incredible knowledge of the area's history. He worked closely with Henry du Pont when the latter created Winterthur, that splendid house-museum outside Wilmington, Delaware, containing the greatest assemblage of American decorative arts in the entire world; and, in truth, Johnston's house here in Kingston could pass for a miniature version of Winterthur. He also is largely responsible for the preservation of Kingston, and his love for the Valley amounts to a fierce passion. "This river has a more diverse history than any but the Nile," he will tell you, and though one is tempted to point out that the Tiber, Seine and Thames also have a story or two, the more you think about it the more you realize that Johnston has a point.

Back to your car, out to Broadway, and follow it to the end, which will take you to **Rondout Creek**, the scene of the action when Kingston was one of the state's most important river ports in the nineteenth century. It was here that the 108-mile-long Delaware & Hudson Canal, completed in 1828, ended, just a short distance from where the creek joins the Hudson. (One of the canal's engineers was John Roebling, later of Brooklyn Bridge fame.) Carrying anthracite coal from Honesdale in northeastern Pennsylvania, the barges would unload here, the coal would be transferred to other boats and then shipped south to New York City.

This, in turn, helped establish Rondout as home base for the steamship and towboat lines, and the city of Kingston prospered. Today the old port is only a shadow of what it once was. A good deal of it was torn down by urban renewal fanatics, but there's a movement under way to restore and revitalize what is left. Although progress may be slow, one definitely senses a feeling of life flowing back. At 41 Broadway, for instance, there's a gallery established by the **Hudson River Maritime Center**, the prime mover behind this mini-renaissance, that is dedicated to recapturing the golden age of the river; the exhibits, small and continually changing, have a homespun charm that makes a stop worthwhile.

The Center also has what they call a "living museum" with frontage on the creek where both traditional and modern boat building and ship rigging are done, plus extensive indoor and outdoor space for exhibits, the most notable being a wonderful old tug, now run aground and rechristened the *William O. Benson,* in honor of Kingston's most famous old river man. Captain Benson, a retired tugboat skipper and extremely talented folk painter, creator of many delightful reproductions of Hudson

This wonderful old tug has found a permanent home at the Hudson River Maritime Center in Kingston and tries desperately to maintain a modicum of dignity under rather trying circumstances.

River steamboats, is also a wonderful person to talk to if you want to learn more about the old days of Rondout and life on the river in general. Short and round, pipe always in hand, he loves to reminisce.

"Twenty-four hours a day you heard steamboat whistles and paddlewheels," he'll tell you. "I got in the business . . . well, my father and brother were in it, and around Kingston in those days there was only about three ways you could make a decent livin', unless your people were well-to-do and sent you to college or somethin'. There was the shipyards. That was hard work. There was the brickyards. That was hard work. And there was the steamboats and the nightboats and the Central Hudson Steamboat Company. And their main terminals was Kingston and New York City.

"Every afternoon at three-thirty, we'd hear that big *Benjamin B. Odell* blow three whistles, or the *Homer Ramsdell* on the way out. You'd see the *Martin* and others come in. You'd see the ferry running between Kingston and Rhinecliff. And then there was tugboats towin' coal boats and scows in and out of the creek all day long.

"At one time it was a very busy place. You never had to go uptown to buy anythin', clothes, hardware, anythin'. There was four or five restaurants, a hotel, newsstands with all the papers and magazines you could want. And there was a railroad station in case you wanted to go up to Oneonta, trolley cars—the Colonial Line and the Broadway Line—and Kingston Point where the pleasure park was. And, of course, there was always some kind of excursion trip goin' outa Kingston.

"You know, I was born the week the *Benjamin B. Odell* made her maiden voyage out of Rondout Crik. My mother liked the lines of the boat so she gave me the middle name of Odell. So I'm prejudiced, but I think she was the most beautiful boat on the Hudson. I remember she'd be leavin' the crik here at eleven on a Saturday mornin'. And just as she got to the mouth, a big Albany nightboat would be deadheadin' back to New York City to bring the crowd out that night and they'd be goin' full speed. So the *Odell* would fall a little behind. I'd stand on a hill to watch her, and when they'd both get to Esopus Light, three miles down the river, where they turned, and just before they went outa sight, well, what do you know, the *Odell* would be goin' out in front, always, the black smoke comin' out of her stacks. Oh, it was a beautiful sight!"

The trolley lines Captain Benson talks about are the reason for the **Trolley Museum**, which provides a pleasant jaunt along Rondout Creek. (Do note the sign "No Parking Trolley Traffic.")

But the real reason to be here is **the best river cruise on the Hudson**, aboard the *Marion T. Budd*. (Hudson River Cruises, phone: 914-255-6515; operates May–October.) It is absolutely not to be missed. This is a family-operated business, and the boat is named after an aunt who helped establish this unforgettable two-hour cruise. Climb aboard. A lovely deep blast on the boat's whistle and you're moving out into the creek, past the spot where the swans nest and the Rondout Light, and then you're on the Hudson.

No matter how often I take this trip my heart always leaps at this moment. The river is so vast. Off to the left, before you turn downstream, the Kingston–Rhinecliff Bridge, so prosaic when you're on it, seems now the slenderest of filaments connecting the two shores. Downstream the tree-covered banks look uninhabited, and the Catskills, gray-blue in the distance, appear almost protective, the natural guardian of the river. (But don't be fooled. Storms can sweep down from these mountains in minutes.) The water is so opaque that it looks solid, only the great undulations of the river giving a hint of its power. One of the family members, Jerry Henne, or sometimes Bill Benson, gives a genuinely interesting, mercifully unobtrusive commentary on what you're seeing.

Really, though, all you need is the experience itself. You can sense the tension being drained from your body, leaving you profoundly relaxed. I've taken many friends, with quite different interests and personalities, along on this trip, and all of them have felt this same letting go.

There is little conversation; the scenery is so majestic that talk seems out of place, except when you see something that you don't want the others to miss, like the Esopus Light on its tiny rocky island—now restored and decorated with witty trompe l'oeil paintings of curtains and pots of geraniums and even a cat in the window—or else glimpses of the great mansions, their dark roofs looming over the trees, their well-kept lawns sweeping down to the water. Sailboats, motorboats, tugs, even freighters seem miles away, the river is so wide, and every few feet the view changes, something new springs into sight, or the light on the water suddenly shifts its patterns as a cloud passes over.

The vistas justify, for once, the word magnificent. You can't help but think of Henry Hudson arriving here over 375 years ago, looking out upon what one of his officers described as "a very good land to fall with and a pleasant land to see" and then remember that you, basically, are viewing the very same thing. No other great river in the world that runs through such highly developed country has remained in such a pristine state as the Hudson right here. It's very moving. "I always think the country is never as interesting as the city," one passenger said to me, "but this is the exception."

That, as I remember, was spoken as the sun was setting behind the Catskills, which someone once said "heave from the valley of the Hudson like the subsiding billows of the ocean

My favorite lighthouse is this one south of Kingston, the Esopus Light, with its trompe l'oeil paintings in the windows, including one of a very worldly cat.

after a storm." No wonder the Hudson River School of painters was the first group of American landscape artists. When you see the valley from this kind of vantage point there can be no question that the scenery is as beautiful as any in the world. And it is our great good fortune that this particular stretch has escaped almost all exploitation and development—so far. If you do only one thing in the Hudson Valley, this, then, should be it. For unless you actually get out on the river you will never understand what it has meant—and still means—to so many people.

The other perfect ending for this day would be dinner at John Novi's **DePuy Canal House** (phone: 914-687-7700) in High Falls, to which Craig Claiborne, world-famous food authority and writer for the *New York Times,* awarded four stars. It is easily the best restaurant in the Valley. More than that, it is one of the great restaurants in the entire nation. (See page 135.)

The handsome stone inn was originally built by Simeon DePuy in 1797, and its fortunes as a hostelry were fully assured when the Delaware & Hudson Canal went into operation in 1828, for the waterway passed within a few yards of the building. Today one of the most romantic features of the setting is the restored lock hard by the restaurant, with its enormous weeping willows looking like an embroidered nineteenth-century mourning picture. When the canal died in 1899 because other means of transportation proved cheaper and quicker and because oil was becoming more and more important, so did the tavern. Then, happily, John Novi bought and restored it, re-

The DePuy Canal House. Should you look through one of these windows you might see diners enjoying some of the best food in the Hudson Valley.

opening it as a restaurant in 1969. Now the place is divided up into small, intimate dining rooms with, at the main entrance, an attractive bar. Guests are also welcome to drop in to the spectacular kitchen and visit with John and his sous-chefs as they work their marvels.

There are five dining rooms. The main one, right behind the bar, seats 18 and has a working fireplace. A slightly smaller room beyond it, once the lock-keeper's quarters, seats 10 and also has a fireplace. Upstairs, there are three more dining rooms, one with a view of the lock, that can take up any overflow or serve as the perfect setting for a private party. Guests are free to wander through all of the rooms, which contributes to the informal, at-home atmosphere.

But there's nothing at home about the food. I remember one dinner in particular. I was coming up from New York City on one of those hot, humid August days that make you feel as if you're trying to breathe and move in damp cotton balls. I had called ahead to John, by now a friend, and warned him I didn't know what time I'd get there. "Don't worry," he replied. "If you miss the regular dinner I'll throw together a soup and salad or you can have some leftovers."

As it happened, we got there just after sunset, and the outdoor lighting made the building an oasis of pleasure. John, a good-looking man with a gentle, friendly manner, came out to say hello, mumbled something about our dinner, and disappeared back into the kitchen after I asked him to decide on the menu for us. A few minutes later a small plate of hors d'oeuvres arrived. Delicious. Next the soup, a light-as-air, beautifully chilled coconut confection with just-picked raspberries. Out of this world. The entrée was fresh shiitake mushrooms in a cream sauce so subtly right it was part and parcel of the mushrooms, with a piece of grilled beef and fresh-from-the-garden buttered vegetables cooked not an instant beyond perfection. For dessert I had more raspberries, my companion an exquisite pastry that John's mother, surely one of the great pastry chefs, had made.

But every meal there is an experience, whether it be Smoked Salmon Ricotta in Pasta with Basil Cream (John does his own smoking) or Quail with Sausage Stuffing on Wild Rice with Plum Sauce or Lobster Bouillabaisse with Saffron Leek Sauce.

To take advantage of seasonal ingredients, the menu is constantly changing, but whatever you order you can rest assured that it will be beautiful to look at, delightful to taste and, oh, so easy to love.

New Paltz

New Paltz is, after Kingston, the most interesting town on the west bank, yet when you drive into it, it's rather disappointing at first glance. Perhaps it's because there's a State University branch here, and somehow I always expect it to look more razzle-dazzle collegiate than it does. And then, too, you can drive straight through the village on Main Street in what seems like two minutes flat without seeing one thing that would make you want to stop. Nevertheless, don't be fooled; New Paltz has much to offer and, including lunch, you can spend a very pleasant half-day here.

What to See and Do

The single most interesting spot is **Huguenot Street**, with its six restored stone houses dating from 1692 to 1705 and allowing the proud and accurate boast that this is "the oldest street in America with its original houses." It's easy to find. Just drive down Main Street, which is also Route 299, toward the Wallkill River. Turn right on Water Street, just before the bridge, follow the road to where it divides, go left and you're there.

I would suggest that you call ahead to the tour office to arrange your tour. (Huguenot Street Tour. Available June to early October, Wednesday–Sunday 10–4. Admission: Varies according to what you wish to see. Phone: 914-255-1660.) As the tour can take as long as two hours, more time than many of us have, I would also suggest that you request yours last no more than an hour. That way you could begin your tour at 11:00 A.M., before many tourists arrive, and then have lunch. Get there a little early, look for the sign for Deyo Hall (it's on your right, and the tour starts there), park your car and then walk back to Huguenot Street. It is indeed a charmer, and this way you'll orient yourself before starting. There is, by the way, a small,

The old French Huguenot Church, built in 1717. Worshippers were called to service by a giant conch shell blown from the tower.

rainbow-hued, old-fashioned country garden that you'll see almost immediately. It's a memorial to one of the benefactors of the street.

As for background, you should know that this land was first settled by twelve Huguenot families in the spring of 1678 and that, by 1792, the street looked basically the same as it does today. (The Reformed Church, dead center on the street, was built in 1839, with additions made later.) The Huguenot families named the settlement New Paltz after Die Pfalz, the Rhenish Palatinate region in Germany that served as their refuge from French persecution. The houses are now protected and owned by The Huguenot Historical Society, whose membership includes dozens of descendants of the original families, presently scattered all over the country.

If you're really pressed for time I would ask to see just two buildings, the French Huguenot Church, still used on special occasions, and the Jean Hasbrouck House. **The French Church** is actually a reconstruction, completed in 1972, of the original built in 1717. It is a small, square, stone building with a steeply canted roof topped by a cupola from which a horn or giant conch shell was blown to summon the worshippers. The whole is quite unlike anything you might see in New England or other parts of New York State. Inside it is extremely simple and very appealing with wide pine-plank flooring, an old French Provincial communion table and elegantly proportioned pews.

The Jean Hasbrouck House is, in my opinion, the best on the street. (Hasbrouck is one of the oldest names in the area, and the local phone book is filled with them.) Not only are the rooms in general better furnished than in any of the other residences, but also the attic has a most spectacular brick chimney that rises about two stories over your head and is supported by a stone wall at the back of the structure and balanced by a frontal beam. It seems odd to rave about a chimney, but this is the only original one in the country, and it makes a powerful impression.

For lunch, continue on for a minute or two down Huguenot Street until you see a sign for the **Locust Tree Inn** on your left. The inn is actually a restaurant set in a stone-and-frame house, the stone part built in 1759 with the frame section added in the early nineteenth century. The food is average—hamburgers, salads, eggs benedict, that sort of thing—but the service is friendly and efficient, the setting very pretty and, anyway, no one ever claimed New Paltz as a center of gastronomy.

Environs of New Paltz

From here drive back to Main Street, turn left, go to South Manheim Boulevard (Route 32 South), turn right, and after about 4 miles you'll see a sign for **Locust Lawn**, a good-looking white-frame Federal mansion built in 1814 by Colonel Josiah Hasbrouck, who fought in the American Revolution. One thing about the Hasbroucks, they never threw anything away, and this house not only harbors superb examples of Duncan Phyfe and Sheraton furniture but also retains all the original documentation for them, such as bills and correspondence, indicating cost and manufacturer. Hasbrouck was rich—real estate was the basis for his fortune—and he was not afraid to spend his money. For me, the single most impressive thing is the

One thing about the Huguenots, they knew how to build a solid house and chimney. These two look forward with confidence to their 300th birthday in a few years.

group of four portraits of family members by Ammi Phillips—and particularly so since the furniture depicted in the paintings can still be seen in the house. John Vanderlyn and Alden Weir are also represented, as well as some of the more mediocre Hudson River School painters, and the house is filled with mementos of the Hasbrouck family, clothes and dolls and books, that give it a very personal quality. It's an excellent documentation of how an upper-middle-class family lived in the early nineteenth century. (Open: June to early October, Wednesday–Sunday 10–4. Admission: $1.50. Phone: 914-255-1660.)

The property also contains a smallish **Wildlife Sanctuary**, pleasant for a leisurely walk along the nature trails. And there's a slaughterhouse, smokehouse and carriage house, where you can wander amid coaches, farm implements and other tools. Far more interesting to me is the tiny, typically Dutch, stone **Terwilliger House**, built in 1738 and across the lawn from the Hasbrouck mansion. Inside there's not all that much to see, although the house itself is a charmer, but at the back of the central hallway there's a window looking out upon a small stream . . . and all of a sudden you're transported back to the eighteenth century. Nothing has changed; the beauty and the wonder remain.

A Drive through Ulster County

In any season, Ulster County presents some of the loveliest scenery in a valley famous for its beauty. Always there is, of course, the river, but the pleasure of this particular drive is the countryside: changing views of the Catskills, vast panoramas from the mountains, lovely old farms with great sweeps of cultivated fields, woods and streams, handsome old houses and small, sleepy villages. If you don't stop anywhere, you could do the circuit in about two hours, but to fully enjoy it I would suggest you plan to make a day of it.

I usually begin from the Kingston–Rhinecliff Bridge, taking Route 209 south toward Ellenville. (If you're coming off the New York State Thruway, take exit 19, then 28W, which also puts you on 209S.) I first like to stop in **Hurley**, a right turn off 209. This wonderful little village was founded in 1662, promptly burned by the Esopus Indians a year later and, finally, resettled in 1669.

Today, what gives Hurley its great charm is the more than dozen eighteenth-century stone houses, all privately owned and lovingly maintained, and the fact that there is practically nothing here that dates from after 1900. The result is a village from the past that has survived intact, and it's pleasant to walk along Main Street looking at the old houses, some with walls as thick as 18 inches. (One, the 1735 Crispell House, just down from School House Lane, has iron spikes in the chimney to catch witches who might decide to enter that way.)

Each year, in early July, Hurley celebrates "Stone House Day," with a tour of about a dozen of the stone houses and the

Why does an ancient cemetery, lonely and abandoned, still exercise a roman-
tic tug at our hearts and impel us to walk among its crumbling stones?

Hurley Reformed Church, as well as the **Hurley Patentee Manor**, originally built in 1696 and then vastly expanded in 1745. (Open: July–Labor Day, daily except Monday, the rest of the year by appointment only. Admission: $1. Phone: 914-331-5414.) There are also a country fair, an antiques show and good, homemade food the same day.

Drive back to 209 and continue south to the village of **Stone Ridge**. There's no one thing in particular to see here, but the village has some lovely buildings, and almost any road off 209 is worth at least a brief excursion to look at the stunning houses and rich, beautifully cared-for land. The area has become a favorite for weekenders who buy houses and summer visitors who rent, bringing in enough money to maintain a heritage that probably never had it so good.

As you leave Stone Ridge, watch for a sign on your left for Rosendale and turn here (213E) to go on to **High Falls**. This is the home of the DePuy Canal House (see page 91), but the tiny village—really a hamlet—has a great deal to offer as well.

First of all, there are two antique centers right off the main road, each representing many different dealers, with a wide selection ranging from junk to some nice country furniture and pottery. And, right next to the Canal House is Lock 16, part of the old Delaware & Hudson Canal system, a handsome, in feeling monumental, tribute to the past. Barges loaded with coal were lowered here, and you can see the six-inch-deep grooves in the Canal House where the ropes burned their way through.

Next, take a look at the falls that gave the town its name, then walk back toward the Canal House, pass it, and turn right when you see a sign for the Mohonk Mountain House. A little farther on, to your left, you will come to the **D & H Canal Museum**. They have a brochure that gives you a plan for a walking tour (about 45 minutes) of the five locks in the area, which can be very pleasant on a nice day, while the tiny museum itself displays canal boat models, photographs and other items from the great days of the D & H; very informal but well done. (Open: May–October, Wednesday–Sunday 11–5. Admission: Donation. Phone: 914-687-9311.)

Baker's Bed and Breakfast, located in this charming 1780 Dutch stone farmhouse, even offers a hot tub. The view is lovely, the rooms attractive, the breakfast first-rate.

Once you're ready to leave, turn right at the Mohonk Mountain House sign. Now you begin the most beautiful section of the drive. Very quickly you're in "real" country, with only a few scattered houses, mostly fields and woods. After a few miles you will come upon a large meadow and, looking up ahead, will see that the road makes a hairpin turn as it begins to climb the mountain. Slow down as you approach the turn and you'll notice a spot where you can pull off the road. Stop, get out, and look back. The view from here is completely unspoiled, with the Catskills for a backdrop, and it's as lovely and tranquil as anyone could ask for; I'd give a lot to have a house right here and watch the changing seasons. Once, in early autumn, I frightened a covey of pheasant here, the perfect finishing touch as I watched their brilliant colors flash away across the meadow.

At the top of the mountain is the entrance to the Mohonk Mountain House (see page 131), the last great survivor from the nineteenth-century era of Hudson River Valley resort hotels. Then, on down the mountain, following the road to its end just outside New Paltz.

Here you will turn right on 299, with the Shawangunk Ridge off to the west. (The tower that you see on the ridge as you drive along is at Mohonk and was erected to honor the memory of Alfred Smiley, who built the hotel.) The scenery is completely different here, a valley with great broad vistas and filled with farms, all surrounded by mountains.

At the end of 299, turn right on Routes 44 and 55, and once again you begin climbing. Soon you will come to areas where you can stop and look back for miles out over the valley and, during warm weather, you will see dozens of cars pulled off on either side of the road, their owners gone to explore the woods and enjoy the loveliness of their surroundings. This is the setting, too, for Lake Minnewaska, a public center for swimming and skiing and allied sports, whose entrance gate you will see on the left.

Farther on, just as you begin your descent, there are two areas where you can again pull off the road to enjoy a vista that extends for 50 miles, both favorite spots of mine. No wonder the father of the Hudson River School, Thomas Cole, on his return from Europe, told people the Alps couldn't hold a candle to the

Catskills. Of its kind, this is one of the loveliest views in the East.

Now you should watch, on the right, for a sign for the Granit Hotel, and once you see it turn right, following the directions for the hotel but passing its entrance. Once again you're in back country. Follow the road to the first Stop sign, in Accord, and turn right again. At the sign for Alligerville, New Paltz and Mohonk, bear left. (It was in Alligerville, by the way, that the peanut-butter sandwich is said to have been invented, based on a recipe brought back from the Caribbean. Who added jelly, I don't know.)

This entire road is lovely, but I do have two favorite spots. One is a stretch bordered on both sides with fragrant pines and a woodland stream on your right that has several tempting swimming holes. The other is a field that ends at the base of the Shawangunk Ridge. Look up and there is the Mohonk Mountain House brooding over the landscape like some fairy castle out of Grimm. At the next Stop sign bear right, and you're on Ulster County Route 6. (If you have time, explore one or two of the fascinating side roads.) Once at the end of this road, you will see a sign showing High Falls to the left, New Paltz to the right. You are back on the road you originally took from High Falls.

Woodstock

It's sad to say, but the charm of Woodstock, though it still remains an arts center with serious pretensions, has been almost obliterated by the tourists who now flock there. The Woodstock Playhouse and the Maverick concerts of chamber music (the oldest series in the country) are still there, of course, and generally still offer first-rate material. And the Woodstock Artists Association, with its changing exhibits of works by local artists, is always worth a visit. But I would strongly suggest that you see or do any of these things during the week; the weekends attract too many people into too small a town, and the result is not pleasant.

The artist tradition goes back to 1902, when Ralph Radcliffe Whitehead, an Englishman out of California with the quintessentially nineteenth-century ideal of founding a center that would work toward the betterment of mankind, chose a spot just north of the town to establish his arts and crafts colony. Then, a few years later, the Art Students League of New York City opened a summer school, and soon musicians, novelists, painters, poets, dancers and the like discovered the considerable charms of the area and began settling in. But along with real talent came, in increasing numbers, the would-be talents and hangers-on, and then, in 1968, the famous—or infamous—Woodstock Festival put the village on the world map and has since caused people to stream into the town who don't know Picasso from Rembrandt and think the only Humperdinck ever is alive and well and singing in Las Vegas. (Oddly enough, the festival was actually held in Bethel, more than 60 miles away, but it was Woodstock that received the curse of fame.)

Since then, the village has tried hard to refurbish its image and it still attracts many interesting people who live outside the town. It still has, too, a pretty setting, an excellent bookstore, some pleasant shops. But the old Woodstock is gone forever, and a weekend night here in summer is more like Sheridan Square in Greenwich Village than the civilized sylvan retreat it once was.

Environs of Woodstock and Kingston

Opus 40   It seems that every time you turn around in Ulster County, there's another poster or brochure for Opus 40, with a picture of some section of this vast, environmental sculpture by the late Harvey Fite. Admittedly, it's a very curious work.

What Fite did was to create his sculpture on the 6-acre site of an abandoned bluestone quarry. (Quarries such as these provided the stone to pave the sidewalks of New York City.) Fite worked on it for 37 years and it was still unfinished when he died in the 1970's. Pathways lead up, down and around pools and trees, and the summit is dominated by a 9-ton monolith.

Quite frankly, I find the whole depressing, an interesting idea gone crazy, but some of the parts do come off. I'm thinking particularly of a section with birch and pine trees that is very beautiful in its contemplative, faintly Japanese way. On the other hand, the somber pools, dark and primeval, definitely do not appeal to me. "A great place for snakes," I overheard one visitor say to another as they peered down into one of them, and that described it perfectly.

There also is a small **Quarryman's Museum** containing
Fite's collection of old quarrymen's tools and furnishings. Opus
40 is near Woodstock and Kingston. It can be hard to find, and
should you decide on a visit, I'd suggest you call for directions.
(Open: June–September, first and third Saturdays 12–5. But this
can vary, so double-check by phone. Admission: $3.00; students
and senior citizens, $2.00. Phone: 914-246-3400.)

DUTCHESS COUNTY:

America's Loire Valley

The Great Houses of the Valley: An Overview

The Hudson Valley estates are unique. Nothing in the country
can equal the variety of these chateaus here, farther north and
in the lower valley. Virginia, it is true, has more than its fair
share of important houses, and New England is a historical gold
mine of domestic architecture. But the sheer number, size, concentration and periods represented in the Valley give the whole
an importance that cannot be rivaled.

The riverfront estates in the northern part of Dutchess
County now form part of a National Register Historic District
and have been described by the Preservation League of New
York State as being "architecturally and historically among the
most magnificent estates in America." Incredibly enough, many
are still in private hands, but three—Franklin Delano Roosevelt's Hyde Park, the Frederick Vanderbilt Mansion, the Ogden
Mills Mansion—are now open to the public. The rest have either been taken over by the state or become semi-public institutions. (The Reverend Sun Myung Moon owns one of the latter,
and I asked one old Hudson Valley denizen what he thought
about the Unification Church for a neighbor. "They've proved
to be—after a shakedown period—reasonably acceptable," he
said.)

I've subtitled this section America's Loire Valley because
that's exactly what it is, a section of the country where our

aristrocracy and nouveau riche—Vanderbilts, Livingstons, Astors, Roosevelts, among others—established great country seats on hundreds of acres and upon which they lavished millions in today's dollars in landscaping, architecture, works of art and furnishings. This extravaganza could never be repeated today.

I've also long been fascinated by how this area has been preserved to such an extraordinary extent (it's almost un-American!) against what must have been intense pressures to sell and develop—and thereby destroy. So I began looking around for someone who could answer my questions, and soon enough found Winthrop Aldrich, a youngish, pleasant man with horn-rimmed glasses who looks like a successful cross between an authentic country squire and an Ivy League professor.

Winthrop and his brother Richard own Rokeby, a house originally built in 1815 for their ancestors General John Armstrong and his wife, Alida Livingston, on Livingston land and one of many nineteenth-century Livingston estates here along the Hudson. John and Alida's daughter Margaret married William Astor, son of John Jacob, who bought the house for the young couple as a wedding present, and enlarged it to its present 45 rooms. Margaret, obviously of a romantic nature, named it Rokeby after a poem by Sir Walter Scott, and the house has remained in the family ever since, the only major change coming in 1895 when Stanford White remodeled part of it.

White with dark-green shutters, an elegant hexagonal tower tucked into one side, the house is large by anyone's standards but also looks homey and lived in, though sadly down at the heels. Winthrop Aldrich, though, is much more than merely a descendant and relative of a good part of the Valley's most ancient families. His mission in life is to preserve this and other places in the state as a national trust, maintaining them for a mixture of private, public and semi-public uses that would fix for all time what is a centuries-old and unique national heritage. It would be an understatement to say that Mr. Aldrich goes about his task with a near-messianic zeal that combines intelligence, wit and good sense.

And it's not easy. The family money is pretty much gone and the Aldriches can't be sure that they'll win. Still, they—and other remaining families like them throughout the Valley— have a sense of *noblesse oblige* that helps keep them going, taking it one day at a time. So far, at least, if they haven't won, they haven't lost, either.

The day I met with Mr. Aldrich he was just ending a discussion with his brother about fixing the porch, whose primary decoration consisted of a pram containing an enormous teddy bear. Once we went inside, though, with the warm sunlight desperately trying to bring back the coloring to an ancient Aubusson rug, the various neglected toys lying in a corner and all the family portraits and old books lent to the interior an oddly timeless aura, perfectly suited to the subject of our conversation.

"This is all I've ever known," Winthrop Aldrich started out saying. "I've lived here and my family's lived here . . . well, at the end of this decade we'll be starting our fourth century of ownership. It's in my blood, the feeling for the land, the feeling for the landscape, the view, the heritage of the region. All of that makes this place very special for me, and by extension the properties next-door and the properties beyond that as well.

"You see, all of the properties along a twenty-mile strip that begin two miles north of Clermont [see page 51] and ends one mile south of the Mills Mansion [see page 118] all stem historically from the marriage of my ancestress Margaret Livingston, who married Judge Robert Livingston, the heir of Clermont, in the 1740's and had ten children. She inherited the Beekman lands and parceled them out to her nine youngest sons and daughters. Her tenth and eldest son, Chancellor Robert Livingston, inherited Clermont and what eventually became the seven properties north of that. And, even today, there is this *cousinage* of Livingston–Beekman descendants, the so-called cadet branch of the family, who settled along the riverbank from Clermont to the south from the 1780's onward.

"It all remained in family hands through the Civil War and was developed into country seats, beginning in the late eighteenth century, to which the family was enormously attached and on which, through their tenant farms, they depended for their incomes. Then it began to change. Some of the land went out of the family, but always the character of the landscape and, to a large degree, the character of the architecture has been respected."

What Mr. Aldrich and his ancestors and his uncles and his

cousins and his aunts—to paraphrase Gilbert and Sullivan—
have done, then, is to create—over several hundred years—a
20-mile stretch of river front that serves as a kind of ongoing
laboratory that illustrates the evolution of landscape design
and domestic architecture by reason of the varying uses—both
horticultural and recreational—to which these estates and
farm lands have been put as some of the family domains have
gradually become converted into public properties. All this cou-
pled with ecologically significant tidal coves, virgin woods and
romantic ravines and waterfalls. It remains unique in the
nation.

"Fortunately so far, the new people buying here respect this
tradition," Aldrich continued. "The ones who are buying the big
estates and investing a lot of money in them seem to be looking
for privacy and even to put down roots. That's what we want.
(By 'we' I mean all of us involved in the conservation of the

*From the terrace of this still-private mansion the view is over the Hudson
to the unspoiled greenery of the west bank.*

Valley.) We don't want the jet set or fad purchaser because they won't stay. We're not geared to meet their needs. Nor do we want the speculators.

"Places like these require continuous care—and a continuous presence, really. So we want people who will get it into their bloodstreams, because it's a very big commitment. And they do come. Perhaps it's serendipity. Not too long ago we had a man who bought two adjacent properties, threw them together and is raising fallow deer. He also owns several other estates in other parts of the country, but now he and his son-in-law and daughter have decided that the Valley is their real home, where they'll raise their family, and they're building a very large house, the first mansion to go up in the mid-Hudson since the Forties.

"You really should see Wilderstein, the Suckley place. It's a good example of what we're trying to do—very, very exciting, a high-style Victorian frame building with a J. B. Tiffany interior and Calvert Vaux landscaping of the grounds. It needs attention, of course, but experts have told us that this property is the most important of all to save.

"Miss Suckley, who is in her nineties, recently turned it over to one of our nonprofit organizations but has retained the right to live there. She's a wonderful person, a distant cousin of FDR, and it was she who raised and gave him Fala, his favorite dog. In any case, she's one of those people who, quietly over the years, realized that what her father and grandfather had created was important, and that if she could live long enough and hold on to it (she is not wealthy), public opinion would finally come around to appreciating it. And she was right. And that's how many of us feel."

(I did go to see Miss Suckley—that afternoon, in fact—and extraordinary is a word that could have been coined to describe this tiny, wiry old lady who looked thirty years younger than she is and walked with a cane only because a broken leg was still mending. There she was, living in this very large, rather looming brown frame house. But as she showed me through the ground-floor rooms, the furniture shrouded and the wallpaper faded even in the golden glow from the Tiffany windows, her belief in its ultimate value, her excitement in the fact that its future was now assured, her memories and her wonderful sense of humor made the house alive and vibrant. I was meeting the last Yankee—lots of backbone, no complaints, a serene knowledge of her exact place in the general order of things. From time to time the property has been opened to the public; various plans are being studied to determine the best use of this property in the future.

Aldrich and I next talked of Olana, Frederic Church's house, which he had also helped to save in 1965 (see page 49). "People said to me, 'Do you really want to save *that?*' Well, we did, a few of us anyway, and now, I believe, it's the most popular state historical site. It's phenomenal. They have waiting lines to get in! And I don't think it's just because it's so exotic, or because it's high on a hill with a spectacular view. It's because it's got a very special message to tell us and now people are ready for it.

"I think we all have an obligation to look particularly carefully at buildings that are seventy-five to a hundred years old and not very popular, figure out which are the best, and try to preserve and save them. It's commonly held that if a property can survive one hundred and ten years—that is, survive to be appreciated by the great-grandchildren—then it's saved. The cycle comes full circle.

"You know, aside from the fact that tastes change, we're all a bit parochial. It's hard to believe that something you've grown up with and are accustomed to seeing in your own backyard is of national importance. So it becomes a matter of education. So we gradually bring in the art-museum curators and the writers and so forth, and then we, the local people, begin to realize that this chair or that view or this landscape arrangement is *unique,* that there's nothing like it in the world, and slowly our values change.

"My point, of course, is that the whole is greater than the sum of its parts; that the whole twenty miles must be protected and must be stabilized. It also has to be recycled in an intelligent fashion or there'll be some disastrous episode of development. If a speculator gets a hold on one of these places and proves that he can make a windfall profit it will, by law, increase the assessed value of all of the other properties—and make it that much harder for the rest of us to hang on and even harder for new people to come in and still pay reasonable prices.

"I like the idea of the area being a mixture of the meticu-

lously restored property open to the public, like Clermont and
Olana, and, nearby, some private property where they're getting along, somehow, as we are here at Rokeby, by fixing only
the porch this summer, the tower next, and then still others like
Wilderstein, which will be a nonprofit venture, involving a lot
of fund-raising, and perhaps ending up as a Victorian study
center.

"Overall, I'm optimistic. Twenty years ago, when my grandmother died here, it really was, my brother and I thought, a
rear-guard action we were taking by remaining. We were sure
these places would be swept away. We were not then, and aren't
now, financially equipped to carry the burden, but this is more
important to us than anything else, certainly more than our
own personal convenience, or taking the long chance that some
other family who bought it or some commercial company that
took it over would respect it as we've tried to.

"We assumed that if we were lucky, we'd be able to hold on
to it for, say, another generation, and if we were doubly lucky,
the same would hold true for the owners of the properties on
either side of us. Now, twenty years have passed and, in effect,
the whole fabric of twenty miles has held because of incremen-
tal solutions to problems. We've lost some buildings, but we
haven't really lost any land. One absolutely fantastic place, for
instance—Wyndclyffe, near Rhinecliff, where Edith Wharton
spent some of her childhood—has now become so dangerous you
can't even approach it. It's probably too expensive, even, to
stabilize as a picturesque ruin. But the land is still there."

(Edith Wharton herself had a slightly different perspective on
Wyndclyffe, which she called Rhinecliff and which belonged to
her father's unmarried sister, Elizabeth: "I can still remember
hating everything at Rhinecliff," she wrote in *A Backward
Glance,* her posthumously published autobiography, "which, as
I saw, on rediscovering it some years later, was an expensive but
dour specimen of Hudson River Gothic, and from the first I was
obscurely conscious of a queer resemblance between the granite
exterior of Aunt Elizabeth and her grimly comfortable home,
between her battlemented caps and the turrets of Rhinecliff.")

After I left Rokeby, I thought: how good they are, how admira-
ble these people, here and in other parts of the country, who are
fighting to keep something for the rest of us that they know to
be important. In many ways, they're pioneering spirits looking

to the future, staking out vital parts of our national heritage to save and develop for our descendants. "A nation can be a victim of amnesia. It can lose the memories of what it was, and thereby lose the sense of what it is or what it wants to be." That's from a historic preservation report prepared in 1966—and that's exactly what the Winthrop Aldriches of this country won't allow to happen.

Houses to Visit

Hyde Park (Springwood) The most famous house in the Valley, this is also the most intensely personal, as if the Roosevelts were expected back at any moment. And that makes it all the more touching. In fact, going through it is a deeply moving experience regardless of one's age or politics. No other presidential house comes off quite so well or as revealingly. Its actual name is Springwood, and it is *in* Hyde Park.

Eleanor Roosevelt published a small booklet on Springwood after the house and grounds were turned over to the U.S. Government. In it she reminisces about her life there and also includes some fragments that FDR wrote, just before he died, as the prelude to a more elaborate account of the estate.

"The Hudson River Valley was in my husband's blood," Mrs. Roosevelt states. "Franklin Delano Roosevelt's family owned land in and around Poughkeepsie and along the banks of the Hudson River for four generations, but even before that his Roosevelt ancestors lived just a bit further down the Hudson River . . . The river in all of its aspects and the countryside as a whole were familiar and deeply rooted in my husband's consciousness."

Roosevelt's father bought the house in 1867—the original structure was built about 1810—after the original family home burned down. This, a typical Hudson Valley house, FDR writes, "was remodeled by my mother and myself in 1915. The central square is substantially the same except that what was known as the south parlor was cut in half. The eastern half being what my mother called 'the snuggery' and the western half is the passage way from the main hall down four or five steps to the big library, occupying the stone addition.

"The architect who redesigned the house in 1915 was Francis W. Hoppin of New York and the contractor was Elliott Brown,

St. James Church, where millionaires and farmers, Roosevelts and Hudson Valley merchants worshipped in harmony. Even King George VI of England, staying at Hyde Park in 1939, attended.

who had built many country houses. He was called 'Tiny' Brown and was center of the Princeton Football Team and weighed about 250 pounds.

"The room in which I was born is the southeast corner of the original tower—the one directly over the snuggery. It also has been cut in half—the eastern half with the fireplace being still a bedroom and the western half part of the hallway going into the new south wing. The furniture in this room is the same as it was before. Until after my mother's death, this furniture had been moved into her room—the southeast corner of the new wing. She moved it out in 1915 and we moved it back at her request after her death."

For Franklin D. Roosevelt, Hyde Park and the Valley were always his real home, and his wife writes that "in the 1930's, Franklin became conscious of the fact that no private home could ever hold, or should ever hold, the interesting collections of various kinds which had come to him while he was the Presi-

dent, in addition to the things which he had personally col-
lected. The war made him realize that one should not put things
of historical interest, and papers of value historically, all in one
place. Modern war could, with one bomb, destroy the Congres-
sional Library with all the records of the past generations. He
wanted his own papers and those of this period to be available
to historians and evolved the idea of giving a piece of land at
Hyde Park on which a library could be erected, which could be
given to the Government of the United States. This was done,
and then my husband told me he had decided to leave the house,
and the land immediately around it, to the United States Government. Of course, he left us the option of living there until our
children died, or until we ourselves gave it to the Government.

"The place he looked upon as the most beautiful was the rose
garden, in which his mother always, up to the last few years of
her life, picked her own roses, and this was where he wished to
be buried."

Mrs. Roosevelt ends by pointing out how particularly pleased
she was that "we were able to leave the rooms exactly as they
had been," and that "the front porch has memories of a very
particular kind, for this is where my husband always stood with
his mother to greet important guests. It is where she always met
him when he arrived for a visit, and on this porch he stood when
his friends and neighbors came to congratulate him after each
nomination and on every election night."

Both the Roosevelts are now buried in the rose garden, and
the Georgian-Federal Revival house would be impressive even
if it had not been the President's home. No one thing stands out,
but the whole is very moving and representative of a certain
manner of living, and of a simpler, less panoplied presidential
era, that strikes very close to the roots of this nation's history.

Nearby is the **library**, a low, handsome, shuttered stone
building crammed with gifts, mementos and personal items of
the President and Mrs. Roosevelt, as well as their personal
papers and the President's private collection on the history of
Dutchess County and the Hudson Valley. It is a treasure trove
for scholars, a fascinating excursion into one of the most important periods in our history for the rest of us. No one should miss
it.

Also on the grounds of Hyde Park is **Val-Kill**. This small
house, built by Franklin in the Dutch style, was Eleanor's

hideaway. "The peace of it is divine," she wrote him. She origi- nally shared it with her two friends, Nancy Cook and Marion Dickerman, later building the nearby furniture factory which for a time produced authentic copies of early American furni- ture and whose purpose was to give the local farmers a means of earning some money during the long winter months.

After the President's death in 1945, Mrs. Roosevelt bought Val-Kill and about 825 acres of farm lands, woods and buildings from the president's estate. Her son John lived in the stone cottage for a while and she in the factory, which she had con- verted into her residence in 1937. This became her sanctuary, the place to which she could retreat to refresh her mind and spirit, until her death in 1962.

Now the small complex has been restored to look exactly as it did at her death.

Springwood is in the town of Hyde Park, on Route 9. The house and library are open seven days a week, March–Novem- ber; Thursday–Monday, December–February; 9–5. Closed Thanksgiving, Christmas and New Year's Day. Admission: $1.50; children and senior citizens, free. This ticket—which cov- ers the Roosevelt house, the library and Val-Kill—also admits you to the Vanderbilt Mansion north of Hyde Park. Val-Kill is open seven days a week, April–October; Thursday–Monday, No- vember and March. Closed December–February. Shuttle bus fees from Springwood: $1.95; children 5–14, $1.10. Phone: 914- 229-9115.

The Vanderbilt Mansion   The Vanderbilts loved to build. And build. And build. No place was safe from their mania: New York City, Newport, Hyde Park, Asheville, Long Island . . . if Julius Caesar came, saw and conquered, the Vanderbilts came, saw and threw down palatial houses in a profusion no other family in this country has ever dreamed of, let alone under- taken.

This one was erected by Frederick William Vanderbilt (1856– 1938), grandson of Commodore Vanderbilt (also fondly known as "The Pirate") who made his initial fortune by dominating the steamboat traffic on the Hudson and then went on to found the New York Central Railroad.

The 54-room, Italian Renaissance structure, almost tiny by Vanderbilt standards, was not the first edifice here; the history

Completed in 1899, the Vanderbilt Mansion cost about $3 million and employed a full-time staff of 60. The grounds here are especially beautiful, and you can stroll down to the river itself to enjoy some splendid views.

of the estate goes back to 1705. In 1795, the first house on this site was built, but more important, it was then that the grounds began to be developed by their then-owner, Dr. Samuel Bard, a process that would continue throughout the nineteenth and well into the twentieth century, eventually making them one of the most beautiful sites in the country. In 1840, John Jacob Astor bought the estate for his daughter, Dorothea Langdon; fifty-five years later her son Walter sold the property to the Vanderbilts.

The Vanderbilts wanted only the best and called in the greatest architectural firm of the time—perhaps in our history— McKim, Mead & White. From 1879 to 1915 this firm designed hundreds of buildings of all types including such masterpieces as the Boston Public Library (probably their greatest creation) and, all in New York City, the masterplan for Columbia University (including the Low Library), the Pierpont Morgan Library and the Villard Houses, now incorporated into the Helmsley Palace Hotel.

William R. Mead was the glue that held the partnership together. Charles F. McKim, probably the greatest of the three and whose sister married the American writer William Dean Howells, also was instrumental in founding the highly prestigious American Academy in Rome and became its first president.

But it is Stanford White people remember today because he got himself murdered in a particularly lurid way. White, a red-headed *bon vivant* and general connoisseur of the arts and of women was also, as J. P. Morgan noted, "always crazy." At one time he had an affair with a very beautiful and very young musical comedy starlet named Evelyn Nesbit. The lady later married Harry K. Thaw, a rich, unbalanced (some said he was a drug addict), pathologically jealous man who was obsessed with the idea that White had done him wrong. On June 25, 1906, Thaw went to the Garden Roof theater of the old Madison Square Garden, a building White had designed, and shot White as he was watching a terrible operetta, *Mamzelle Champagne,* which managed to run for 59 more performances thanks to the ensuing scandal. There's a 1955 movie, *The Girl in the Red Velvet Swing,* about the whole affair that shows up from time to time on late-night television. Don't take it too seriously, but it's an hour or two that's fun, and stars Ray Milland as White, Farley Granger as Thaw, and Joan Collins as Evelyn Nesbit.

But back to the Vanderbilts. McKim, Mead & White soon discovered the Langdon mansion could not be remodeled because of structural problems and that, instead, the building had to be razed.

Down it came, and by 1899 the new house was ready, at a cost of just under $3 million and requiring a full-time estate staff of 60. (The interior design, by the way, was partially done by Ogden Codman who, with Edith Wharton, had written *The Decoration of Houses* [1897]. Among other things, their book established the principle that architecture and design cannot be separated, with the logical corollary that ornament is not to be used for its own sake but only as a part of the architectural whole; in essence, this meant that careful consideration of proportion, symmetry, order and harmony are vital to the success of any room. Wharton and Codman's primary role models were taken from French architecture and furnishings of the eighteenth century. From the day of its publication the book became an instant classic, so important that it radically changed American taste in decoration and has indeed shaped general concepts of interior design up to the present.)

Frederick Vanderbilt occupied the mansion until his death in 1938, but only from Easter to the beginning of July, and then again in the fall. The Vanderbilts were not alone in this ritual; most of the great estate holders followed the same pattern of being in New York City for the late fall and winter season and then, in the summer, either moving on to Newport or another resort or else traveling to Europe.

Today, the house is perfectly maintained and appears generally the way it was when the Vanderbilts lived there. It's very beautiful, but so formal that it seems more like a public building to receive in than a home. In many ways, of course, that's exactly what it was. Best of all, the guide takes you in and then leaves you alone to look at the rooms in peace. None of that "and this is the writing desk circa 1796 that Mrs. So-and-So used every day to write thank-you notes and fire servants" stuff that can drive you crazy. (Something that particularly fascinates me is that there are several tapestries bearing the coat of arms of the Medicis. Did Frederick Vanderbilt wish to imply a family resemblance?)

The most perfect room is Mrs. Vanderbilt's bedroom, for which Codman is responsible and which is exquisite despite one element, the bed, that to me is so naïvely pretentious it's almost touching. The general plan was to recreate a French queen's bedroom of the Louis Quinze period. The offending bed, huge and canopied, is surrounded by a rail before which, in France, the courtiers would have gathered for the queen's levee. I would bet none of Mrs. Vanderbilt's guests ever saw *her* en déshabillé. Still, the room is extremely elegant, a model of what Codman and Wharton preached in their book, with its French furniture, wood-paneled walls with inset paintings, and superb detailing such as the hand-embroidered silk covering the wall at the head of the bed.

The estate grounds, developed over almost two centuries since the time of Dr. Bard back in 1795, are just as interesting as the house. For instance, there are about 40 species and varieties of trees (most are marked) including a gargantuan gingko, one of the largest in the country. And, along the north drive on the way out of the estate, there is a view of the Hudson, the Shawangunk Mountains (to the west) and the Catskills (to the north) that is among the most beautiful in the Valley.

Still, my favorite spot is down by the river itself. As you leave on the north drive, there is a road off to the left that takes you down the hill, over the railroad tracks, and out to the site where the Vanderbilt yachts once docked. Wander along the shore here. The vista, constantly changing as you move from place to place, is always breath-taking, and, once again, there's that special feeling of serenity and peace that only this river can create to such haunting effect.

The Vanderbilt Mansion lies north of Hyde Park on Route 9. Open daily 9–6 summer, 9–5 winter, except for Thanksgiving, Christmas and New Year's Day. Phone: 914-229-9115. Admission: $1.50; children and senior citizens, free. This ticket also admits you to the Roosevelt house and library in Hyde Park.

The Mills Mansion   Yet another Livingston estate, this one served as the model for the Trenor's estate, Bellomont, in Edith Wharton's masterpiece, *The House of Mirth*. (I wonder how the Mills liked her description of their library: "A few family portraits of lantern-jawed gentlemen in tie-wigs, and ladies with large head-dresses and small bodies, hung between the shelves buried with pleasantly shabby books: books mostly contemporaneous with the ancestors in question, and to which the subsequent Trenors had made no perceptible additions. The library at Bellomont was in fact never used for reading...." They would have been more pleased, I suspect, with her description of the grounds in all their "opulent undulations.") The estate goes back to 1792 and a sister of Chancellor Robert Livingston (see page 52), Gertrude by name. She was married to Morgan Lewis, a prominent New Yorker who had been General Horatio Gates' chief of staff at the Battle of Saratoga and would later go on to become chief justice of the New York Supreme Court (1801–4) and governor of the state (1804–7). The Lewises' first home burned to the ground in 1832, but they promptly built a new one in the Greek Revival style. (It's odd that Greek Revival lasted only a short time in domestic architecture yet continued well into the twentieth century for our public buildings.)

This structure is the core of the present French Renaissance-inspired building designed by McKim, Mead & White (see page 115) at the request of Ogden and Ruth Livingston Mills and completed in 1896. (Mills' parent had made a fortune in California in banking; Ogden enjoyed the fruits of his father's labors.) The house remained in the family until 1937 when the only son, Ogden Livingston Mills, one-time Secretary of the Treasury, died, and his sister decided to give the house and its surrounding 200 acres to the state.

This mansion is larger than the Vanderbilt's—65 rooms— and in many ways far more interesting. First of all, the core of the old house gives a nicely unbalanced feeling to the whole; you immediately sense that there may be some surprises awaiting you instead of the usual matching rooms, north and south, leading leadenly off a central hall. And there are. The most beautiful of these is the dining room, long and splendid with large, framed tapestries set off against gray-green marble, its western windows overlooking the Hudson and the mountains. It has to be one of the great formal rooms of its period. Not a must perhaps, this house, but very rewarding if you're at all in-

The back of the Mills Mansion, designed by McKim, Mead & White. The dining room, though sadly down-at-the-heels, remains one of the great private rooms from the late nineteenth century.

terested in nineteenth-century architecture and decoration.

The Mills Mansion is north of Hyde Park and the Vanderbilt Mansion and about 5 minutes off Route 9 (there's a sign) in Staatsburg. Mansion and grounds are open from Memorial Day weekend through Labor Day, Wednesday–Saturday, 10–5; Sunday, 1–5. From Labor Day through the last Sunday in October, Wednesday–Saturday, 12–5; Sunday, 1–5. Phone: 914-889-4100. Admission: Free.

Most of the estate is now part of the **Mills–Norrie State Park**, which has a boat basin, tent-trailer sites, fishing, golf and picnicking facilities as well as nature and hiking trails. Phone: 914-889-4646.

A Drive through Dutchess County

Once you get off Route 9, the scenery in Dutchess County can be very beautiful, mostly rolling land covered with rural property and, in particular, horse farms. For various reasons—mainly tax incentives—the entire Valley has become a major horse-breeding area with more than a hundred horse farms, fifty of them in Dutchess County alone. At the same time, horse-raising has turned into such a big business that it's listed among the larger industrial contributors to New York's tax base. Fortunately, you don't have to know a thing about taxes or horses to appreciate the beauty of these farms with their seemingly endless brown or white fences streaking the landscape.

Wine-making, too, is important here, and the vineyards on the hillsides seem to be almost as common a sight as the apple orchards or cornfields surrounding the small towns and villages that dot the county.

This drive is designed to take you through a little bit of everything so that you can get a feel for the region. Depending on the time you wish to spend, you could do it in 2 or 3 hours or you can make a day of it.

Begin in Rhinebeck (see page 124), right in the heart of the village where Route 308 meets Route 9, almost directly across from the Beekman Arms (see page 136). Follow 308 (it's also East Market Street here) and take it to the sign for 9G South, enjoying in the meantime the vintage houses, dating from pre-Revolution to late-Victorian, most of them kept in prime condition.

After a mile or so on 9G you will see a sign, on your left, for Slate Quarry Mill and Stanfordville. Turn off and follow this road to the sign for Schultzville and Clinton Hollow, where you will turn right. Go through Schultzville, which seems to consist of a small, pretty clapboard nineteenth-century grange and, on a triangle, a country store and a couple of houses. You will then climb a small hill, and just over the brow will be a sign on your left for Schultzville Road. Part dirt, part paved, this wonderful road will take you through a lovely wooded section, full of deer and other wild animals, that is country primeval.

After 5 or 10 minutes you'll come upon a sign for **Clinton Vineyards**, a small winery that produces the best white wine (a Seyval Blanc) on this side of the Hudson. Ben Feder, proprietor of the vineyard, is a transplanted New York City graphics designer who first started raising cattle, quickly got bored with that and decided to take a gamble on a vineyard. (Oddly enough,

By American standards the Valley is ancient in its history—hence this Greek Revival church now standing alone in the middle of the woods.

the best vineyard on the west bank, Ben Marl, is also owned by
an ex-graphics designer, Mark Miller.) That was back in 1977,
and Feder's venture has paid off handsomely, his first major
break coming when a *New York Times* critic wrote that his was
an unusually good wine. Within no time Clinton Vineyards was
sold out of its stock, its reputation firmly established, and today
it is served at such New York City establishments as The Four
Seasons (noted for its excellent selection of American wines)
and "21." Ben Feder, a friendly, gregarious man, welcomes
guests, but this is a small operation, and you must call ahead
to set up an appointment (phone: 914-266-5372).

From here, go to the end of Schultzville Road and turn right.
Almost immediately you're in Clinton Corners, a sleepy little
village where you will get on, for a short time, the Taconic
Parkway going south. Get off at the Millbrook exit (U.S. 44), and
follow 44 into **Millbrook**. (If it's lunchtime, you may wish to
stop off at the Cottonwood Inn, just a minute or two beyond the
sign for Route 82 and on your left. This pretty white frame
Victorian building with black shutters has a standard, good-
enough lunch menu, and makes a pleasant break—there's no
better place in Millbrook.)

As you turn left on 44 to go into the village, the buildings
on your right are the remains of the now-defunct Bennett
Junior College. Once in the village, 44 becomes a main
street. Park your car anywhere along here. The minute you
start examining the stores along this street, you'll discover that
you've lit on a swarm of antique shops. Dozens of dealers are
represented in the different buildings or antique malls on either
side of the street, and you can easily spend an hour or two
walking through and just looking at the merchandise; it covers
every conceivable interest and taste, from furniture to porcelains to paintings to old clothes to bric-a-brac, with a wide
range of prices beginning at only a few dollars. If you collect, or
are looking for any one thing in particular, just ask. There's
bound to be at least one of whatever it is. And don't be afraid
to bargain. In all these malls the prices are 10 to 20 percent
higher than they'll actually take, I've found.

At the same time, there's only one top quality shop, which sits
regally off by itself on 44 (phone 914-677-5511 for directions) and
is called "Joyce Harris Stanton, Antiques and Interiors." Ms.

The star of Schultzville, this charming clapboard grange is right out of a Norman Rockwell cover for the Saturday Evening Post.

Stanton has a small selection, basically of eighteenth and nineteenth century English furniture, but it's good, and after the hubbub of the malls, it's nice to stop in here for some peace and quiet. The whole experience is one you'll enjoy, and it is hard to walk away empty-handed.

Millbrook has one other claim to your attention. It was here that Peter Piper picked a peck of pickled peppers. James Kirke Paulding, the creator of that deathless line, was Secretary of the Navy under fellow New Yorker Martin Van Buren. Aside from this immortal series of p's, Paulding is primarily remembered for defending sail against steamships. Fortunately, we were not at war at the time.

Once you're ready to go on, retrace your drive back to the sign for Route 82, and go north on this to relax and just enjoy the scenery. For a good part of the way it is carefully tended farm country, with some handsome old houses and cornfields stretching out toward the mountain range to the west. It's very rural, very pleasant, and hasn't changed much since the 1800's.

When you enter Pine Plains, go left on Route 199. Soon the
scenery shifts to woods and small ponds and, as you proceed,
pretty views down into the valleys. In Rock City, which makes
Schultzville look like a metropolis, bear left on Route 308; in
about 15 minutes you'll be back in Rhinebeck.

I should tell you one other thing. There are lots of dirt roads
in this area, particularly around Schultzville, all great fun to
explore. Don't hesitate to go off on one of them. Get lost, even.
In its own quiet way this can prove quite rewarding; you're
bound to come across something of great beauty, a landscape or
a building or a view, that will stay forever in your memory.

Other Places to Visit in Dutchess County

Rhinebeck   This small village of just over 2,500 people was
founded by the Dutch in 1686 but received its present name
around 1713 from a group of German settlers, refugees, in re-
membrance of their homeland river ("beck" means cliffs).

These settlers, part of a much larger group that had dispersed
to other parts of the Valley and further south to New York City
and New Jersey, had a particularly tragic background. Crushed
by centuries of wars and taxes, the peasants of the Rhine Valley
were all too ready to listen to English agents who raved to them
about the wonders of America. Within the years of 1707 to 1709
more than 11,000 of them had arrived in England, waiting to be
sent on to the New World. Eventually about 2,800 embarked,
the largest single migration during the colonial period, on a
voyage that would take them months. When they arrived in
New York, 1,800 were dispatched 100 miles upriver to produce
naval stores, particularly tar, for the English. Unfortunately,
the whole project collapsed after several extremely difficult
years, and the settlers were abandoned by the English to get on
as best they could. (One of them, by the way, was John Peter
Zenger (1697–1746), founder of the New York *Weekly Journal,* a
newspaper highly critical of the British colonial government. In
1734 Zenger was arrested and tried for libel. Defended by Alexander Hamilton, he was finally acquitted—on the then-revolu-
tionary defense that truth was no libel. Thanks to Zenger—and
to Hamilton, of course—freedom of the press became a funda-
mental right, one more step toward breaking the dominion of
Mother England over the colonies.)

The Delameter House with its fanciful gingerbread, spreading across and around and up and down. A confectioner's delight, good enough to break off a piece to munch on as you continue your walk down the street.

For a village so small, it's something of a surprise to discover that Rhinebeck has a railroad station, on the river and two miles west, in Rhinecliff. All becomes clear, however, when you learn that so many private railroad cars began coming up here after the Civil War, bearing the heavy freight of wealth headed for the mansions north and south of the village, that Colonel John Jacob Astor IV and his cronies insisted upon having a convenient place to disembark.

These same people had magnificent gardens and greenhouses, and as the mansions went into their long, gentle decline in the twentieth century, the gardeners once employed by the wealthy began operating their own commercial greenhouses. They soon found that violets did particularly well here, and before long, there were acres and acres of them—the largest violet market in America, with Rhinebeck becoming known as "Violet Town." But then violets grew unfashionable in the 1920's and '30's; so these days it's anemones that are raised here for the commercial markets.

In many ways, this series of failures has been nothing but good news for Rhinebeck since it's meant that there was no call to tear down the old buildings to throw up bigger, more commercial ones for expanding needs. So today what you see is an intact nineteenth-century village—with a few even older buildings—and because Rhinebeck remains prosperous and concerned about its heritage, it is very well maintained as a National Historic District.

The whole village is worth touring—on foot since it's so small —but three particular buildings I'm very fond of perhaps sum up the special quality that gives the town its distinction.

The Delameter House (1844), just up Montgomery Street (Route 9) from the village's only stoplight, is the quintessential example of an American Gothic house and is so fanciful that it looks like a toy. It was designed by Alexander Jackson Davis, the country's most famous architect of domestic Gothic and whose masterpiece is Lyndhurst (see page 181). It has everything—a wonderful central gable, gingerbread woodwork so exuberant it seems more important than the house, diamond-paned windows, over-tall chimney stacks, projecting bay windows. And, best of all, you can stay there, as it is now owned by the Beekman Arms (see page 136).

The Dutch Reformed Church (1809), on Route 9 and South Street, is a successful hodgepodge of styles (the windows are Georgian on the front, Gothic on the sides, for instance) and materials (brick and stone was a compromise between the rich and poor parishioners: the rich could afford brick, the poor only stone).

Finally, there's a high-style **Victorian mansion** on West Market Street, about two blocks from the traffic light, that has been so beautifully restored it could serve as the model for a Christmas card. It's perfect of its kind, a wonderful turret with an oeil-de-boeuf window, widow's walk, mansard roof, a splendid arched door. When *New Yorker* cartoonist Charles Addams saw it he said, "Why, that's my family house. That's what I've been drawing all these years."

Old Rhinebeck Aerodrome   Just a few miles north of Rhinebeck, off Route 9 on Stone Church Road, the Aerodrome can be a lot of fun. Although it attracts large crowds, the last time I was there it was empty, and as I got out of my car the first thing I heard was a trumpet going crazy, a bit bizarre at ten in the morning. The site is wired for sound, and the music is of World War I vintage. From here it's *not* a long way to Tipperary.

You enter across a covered bridge decorated with photos of pilots, "Germans" and "Americans," who go up in the air each Saturday and Sunday and hold mock air fights to delight the spectators. Along the grass landing strip is an extraordinary lineup of antique planes, and on the other side are prop houses (the Germans have "Das Badz Boyz," the French the "Hotel de Paree") that are used in the shows. You also can take a jaunt in an open-cockpit plane, "high or low, fast or slow, any way you

This Lutheran church near Rhinebeck was built in 1786 by German refugees from the Palatinate. Now it stands opposite the entrance to the Rhinebeck Aerodrome.

want to go" as the barker will tell you, over the Hudson Valley.

When you leave and are about to turn onto Route 9, do note the Lutheran church directly opposite. It was built in 1786 by German Palatinate refugees.

The Aerodrome puts on air shows from mid-May to October on Saturday and Sunday at 2:30 P.M. Admission: Adults, $5; children 6–10, $2. The Aerodrome itself is open daily from mid-May to October, 10–5. Entrance fee for adults, $1.50; children 6–10, $1. For airplane ride prices call 914-758-8610.

Bard College   About 20 minutes north of Rhinebeck on Route 9G, this small liberal-arts college founded in the mid-nineteenth century has a charming 600-acre campus that is, in large part, made up of former Hudson River estates.

As you enter the gates, turn right following the sign directing you to Admissions. This tiny, white hexagonal building, worth noting in its own right, once served as the gatehouse to an estate called Blithewood, which originally belonged to John Bard, founder of the college. It was the creation of architect Alexander Jackson Davis (see page 182) and was built in either the 1830's or '40's (dates vary). Turn right here.

Further on, to your left, is a group of modern buildings that includes the **Edith C. Blum Art Institute** which offers changing exhibits of excellent quality in well-planned gallery spaces. (Open all year, Tuesday–Saturday 10–5, Sunday 1–5. Closed Monday. Phone: 914-758-6822. Admission: Free.) Continue on the same road and you'll see a large, very striking Neoclassic mansion that replaced the original Blithewood house about 1900 and is now a dormitory. It's nice to get out here and wander, catching glimpses of the Hudson. If you should then decide to explore the main part of the campus, be sure to note the library, built for the college in 1893 in the form of a classic Greek temple; rather peculiar and chilly on the Hudson.

Vassar College Art Gallery   Vassar, on Raymond Avenue in Poughkeepsie, has an extensive and major art collection, particularly a superb group of Hudson River School paintings. Unfortunately, the Art Gallery has very little space to show it in. Still, a visit is worthwhile for their temporary exhibits are always thoughtfully presented and original in conception, while whatever is on display from the permanent collection should give you an idea of its overall quality. If you have a special interest that is represented in their holdings, you can make a study appointment. Catalogues are available of the different collections, and the phone number is 914-452-7000.

The gallery is open Monday–Saturday 9–5, Sunday 1–5, during the school year. Other times are by appointment only.

Locust Grove   This is the former home of Samuel F. B. Morse, an artist who ended up being more famous for inventing the telegraph than for any of his paintings. Morse bought it in 1847 and created the Tuscan villa you're looking at with the help of Alexander Jackson Davis (see page 182). Sold in 1901 to the Young family, it was a descendant of this family who, in 1975, established a generous endowment to maintain the house and grounds as a historic site. There are pleasant hiking trails through the woods and an attractive garden, but I find the interior of the house to be a hodgepodge of uninteresting furniture and such trivia—to me, anyway—as doll, fan and costume collections. In fairness, though, it is an excellent way to see how people lived in the late nineteenth century, and among the dross are some treasures.

Locust Grove is open from late Memorial Day weekend through September, Wednesday–Sunday 10–4. It lies about 2 miles south of the Mid-Hudson Bridge in Poughkeepsie on Route 9. Phone: 914-454-4500. Admission: Adults, $3; children 7–16, $1.

Revolutionary War Sites   The area south of Poughkeepsie is rich in Revolutionary War sites and there are at least three, each within a few minutes' drive of the others, that might interest some of you: the 1709 **Madam Brett Homestead** (open mid-April to mid-November, Friday–Sunday 1–4); the 1732 **Van Wyck Homestead Museum** (Memorial Day–Labor Day, Saturday and Sunday 1–5); and **Mount Gulian**, 1730–40, also known as the Verplanck Homestead (May–December, Wednesday and Sunday 1–5). All three are near Beacon, which is south of Poughkeepsie. Although they aren't exactly dull, none is worth a detour unless you are a real Revolutionary War buff.

Of the three, I found the most interesting to be the Madam Brett Homestead. (In Beacon at 50 Van Nydeck Avenue. Phone:

Mt. Gulian, Baron Von Steuben's headquarters during the Revolution and the birthplace of the Order of Cincinnati, whose first president was George Washington.

914-831-6533. Admission: Adults, $2; children under 19, 50¢.) During the Revolution, the house held commissary supplies for the American Army and was supposedly visited by Washington and Lafayette. It's a good example of Dutch architecture from the early eighteenth century and has some interesting furnishings and a pretty garden.

The Van Wyck Homestead served as part of an enormous supply depot for the Americans and now has changing exhibits based on the colonial period. (At the junction of Route 9 and I-84 just south of Fishkill. Phone: 914-896-9560. Admission: Adults, $1; children 7–12, 50¢.)

The present Mount Gulian is a copy of the original 1740 building in which General Friedrich von Steuben of the American Army forces had his Hudson Valley headquarters. Perhaps the most interesting event associated with Mount Gulian is that the Society of the Cincinnati was founded here. This fraternal group of American officers from the Revolution who had served for at least three years with the Continental Army included a host of notables, and George Washington was its first president. (In Rombout Village off Route 9D at the northern edge of Beacon. Phone: 914-831-8172. Admission: adults, 50¢; children, 25¢.)

Where to Stay and Eat

Ulster County
Area Code: 914

Where to Stay

Mohonk Mountain House, New Paltz 12561. Phone: 255-1000 (In New York City: 233-2244). Open all year. Rates vary; reserve well in advance. Credit cards accepted.

In the nineteenth century, the Valley was famous for its enormous and splendid resort hotels, many with extraordinary views of the river, all set amid great natural beauty. Visitors from around the world would travel to them, write about them, paint them, praise them—and sometimes condemn them.

Today only Mohonk, which opened in 1870, remains, an enormous Victorian pile at the end of an exquisite blue-black lake that's 1,200 feet above the Valley. Founded by twin brothers Albert and Alfred Smiley, the hotel still is owned by the family, and now has just over 300 rooms.

The grounds are spectacular—all 7,500 acres of them. The gardens are mature and grand, specimen trees dot the lawns, 30 miles of bridle trails take you through the general magnificence and, what's more, you can see 5 states from Mohonk's tower. Golf, tennis, hiking, skating, skiing, swimming, riding, concerts . . . you name it, they've got it. Some people consider this one of the most beautiful hotel sites on earth, and I would agree.

So why do I dislike it? Probably because it makes me feel as though I'm in a carefully regulated prep school where I'm treated well but watched too closely to see that I don't misbehave or shame my family. You enter Mohonk through a lodge gate from which a staff member calls to confirm that you are indeed a guest, not a crasher. Then you drive along a carefully maintained road, liberally dotted with "Slowly and Quietly, Please" signs until, after 5 minutes or so, the hotel heaves in sight. Attendants sweep you off to the parking area, gently but firmly. Gentle and firm is the rule here, a remnant, no doubt, of the Quaker background of the Smiley family.

The dining room offers panoramic views, but guests at tables by the windows often pull down the shades against the setting sun. There is no bar, although you can have drinks at your table. There is no smoking. A selection of bottles and condiments stands guard on each table, my own all-time favorite being a jar of Postum, an item I'd thought long extinct. The food is plain, plentiful and cooked for American taste buds that stopped developing circa 1930. Rooms are old-fashioned, reasonably comfortable if rather homely, but they do look out on breathtaking scenery.

Maybe I'm being overly harsh, although I'm not alone in my feelings. It certainly is worth seeing, and I would suggest that you first go there for a meal or as a day guest (there's an admission fee). That way you can enjoy some of the hotel's real attractions while deciding for yourself. I should also add that it's a good place to bring children because there are so many planned and supervised activities for them. The resort also has special programs throughout the year—a tennis week, a garden week, music weeks, a mystery fans week (might be fun, that), and so forth—some of which may interest you. If so, write and ask for their special brochures.

Bed & Breakfast Inns

Ulster County has more than a dozen Bed & Breakfast lodgings, and two of them are very attractive indeed. This concept of private-home owners renting rooms and supplying breakfast to tourists originated in England, spread to California and then bounced back east. Basically, anyone with an extra bedroom can do it and, in fact, some B & B's do have only one room available. Others, however, are really small inns that are run in a thoroughly professional manner.

Depending on your taste, there can be drawbacks. For instance, you may not wish to face other people across a table in the morning no matter how good the breakfast may be. And, in almost all cases, bathrooms are shared. One other note: The better ones are extremely popular throughout the year, and it is imperative that you reserve well in advance. Here follows an alphabetical listing of the ones I like. None accept credit cards.

Astoria Hotel, 25 Main Street, Rosendale 12472. Phone: 658-8201. Eight rooms. Rates: About $40 for a double.

Rosendale is a sleepy little town near New Paltz at the conjunction of Routes 213 and 32. Jeannine Gleissner, proprietor of this, the only real hotel in the group, is one of France's most appealing exports and has done an excellent job in restoring and running the inn.

The Astoria was built in the early 1860's, an attractive brick building with a welcoming porch, when Rosendale was not only a center for cement mining but also a stop-off on the Delaware & Hudson Canal. The guest rooms are nicely furnished and comfortable, and each has its own kitchen and bathroom. You can have a breakfast in your room of fresh orange juice and coffee, excellent croissants and buttered baguettes plus imported jams. There is also a gourmet food shop.

Baker's Bed and Breakfast, RD #2, Box 80, Stone Ridge 12484. Phone: 687-9795. Five rooms. Rates: About $50 for a double. Just beyond Stone Ridge but off Route 209 on Old King's Highway. Highly recommended.

By anyone's standards this, one of the two best in the county, is a particularly pretty inn. Located in a 1780 Dutch stone farmhouse and operated by Doug Baker, the place is set on a hill with a lovely view to the Shawangunk Mountains and a very pretty field across the road. There's a hot tub here, and the bedrooms are not only comfortable but are also attractively furnished, with homespun coverlets and handsome antique bureaus, beds and carpets. Breakfast is elaborate, vastly filling and delicious. It deserves its own special mention for the first-rate quality.

Captain Schoonmaker's 1760 Stone House, Box 37, High Falls 12440. Phone: 687-7946. Seven rooms. Rates: About $50 for a double. On Route 213 between High Falls and Rosendale. Highly recommended.

Julia and Sam Krieg took this falling down old house and turned it into a charmer in no time. Both have energy to burn. And, when they were done, they turned to the barn and created three large new bedrooms. The four rooms in the main house are on the smallish side, but one does have a working fireplace. I prefer the barn, though, with its high-ceilinged rooms overlooking the Coxing Kill, a little stream that meanders through the property. Breakfast here features home-baked breads, various fruit danishes, bacon, eggs, fresh fruit compote, fruit juice and coffee.

House on the Hill, Box 86, High Falls 12440. Phone: 687-9627. Five rooms. Rates: About $50 for a double. On Route 213 in High Falls.

Shelly and Sharon Glassman, a pleasant and relaxed couple, do their best to make you feel right at home in this modest and comfortable 1825 house, and both usually involve themselves in preparing your breakfast, which, in the winter, is served by the fireplace and, in all seasons, usually consists of fresh fruits, lovely home-baked breads and muffins and so forth.

Ujjala's Bed and Breakfast, 2 Forest Glen Road, New Paltz 12561. Phone: 255-6360. Three rooms. Rates: About $50 for a double. South of New Paltz and just off Route 208S.

This 1910 house, set among old fruit trees, is as different from the others as night is from day. So is Ujjala, who is into stress management and body therapy and will make an appointment with you, should you desire, for a session in Shiatsu or massage. The rooms are, well, different (one is black and beige, rather startling in a Victorian house), but Ujjala could not be nicer and serves a breakfast of fresh fruits, eggs, home-baked breads and coffee—or herbal teas. There also is an afternoon tea that is included in the price, and she will accommodate any requests you may have for special diet foods.

Where to Eat

The first two restaurants below—DePuy Canal House and Schneller's—in their very different ways offer as good food as you will get anywhere and are very highly recommended.

DePuy Canal House,   High Falls. Phone: 687-7700. On Route 213. Credit cards accepted. (See page 91).

My favorite restaurant in the Valley. Prix-fixe dinners (about $40) and à la carte selections available. Unless you have a very large appetite, stick with the à la carte selections. Open Thursday-Saturday, 6–10; Sunday, 3–9. Weekend brunch, 11–2. Reservations a must.

Schneller's Restaurant, 61–63 John Street, Kingston. Phone: 331-9800. No credit cards accepted. (See page 83.)

Excellent home cooking with a German bias. Homemade breads, sausages, meats, pâtés and desserts. I prefer it at lunch, looking out the windows of the upstairs dining room, but dinner is first rate, too, and the prices are very reasonable. Lunch: Monday–Saturday, 11:30–4. Dinner: Wednesday and Thursday, 5–9; Friday and Saturday, 5–10. Reservations recommended on the weekend.

The Bear Cafe and The Little Bear,   Bearsville. Phone: 679-9427 and 679-9497, respectively. On Route 212 near Woodstock. Credit cards accepted.

The Bear Cafe has an international dinner menu—lobster, steak and so forth—as well as vegetarian dishes. It's good enough, but the attraction here is lunch on the terrace by a stream. Very pleasant on a summer day. Reasonably priced. Breakfast and lunch are served from 10–4, dinner from 4–11 every day but Wednesday. Reservations suggested for dinner.

The Little Bear is the surprise; it's a good Chinese restaurant with a wide selection of dishes from different provinces. Open daily, 12–12. Reservations are necessary, but you still might have to wait on weekends.

Deanie's,   Woodstock. Phone: 679-6508. At Routes 212 and 375. Credit cards accepted.

A Woodstock classic with an unextraordinary menu but generally well-prepared food. There's a porch for summer dining and entertainment every night but Monday. Closed Tuesday, open every other day 4–2 A.M. Reservations suggested.

La Duchesse Anne,   Mt. Tremper. Phone: 688-5260. Intersection of Route 212 and old Route 28. About 20 minutes from Woodstock. Credit cards accepted.

A crowded, noisy, dark but friendly restaurant that supposedly specializes in Breton food but is really basic French. Fair. Closed Tuesday. Dinner on weekdays, 6–10; Saturday, 6–10:30; weekend brunch, 10–2. Reservations suggested.

L'Auberge 32, 240 Boulevard (on Route 32), Kingston. Phone: 331-4386. Credit cards accepted.

Now here is an honest restaurant, totally unpretentious and serving a basic French menu with proper care and attention to the ingredients and preparation. The result is a meal that you always can count on to be a satisfying experience. Closed Sunday. Lunch: Monday–Friday, 12–2. Dinner: Monday–Thursday, 5–9; Friday and Saturday, 5–10. Reservations suggested on weekends.

Top of the Falls, High Falls. On Route 213. Phone: 687-7565. Credit cards accepted.

A sophisticated menu that sometimes makes it, sometimes doesn't, but a pretty spot, attractively decorated, and appeals especially to the weekend crowd. Open daily. Dinner: 6–10. Sunday brunch: 12–3. Reservations needed.

Dutchess County
Area Code: 914

Where to Stay

Good inns are at a premium in Dutchess County. In fact, there are only three, and two of these, Troutbeck and the Old Drover's Inn, are so far east of the river as to be almost at the Connecticut border. Nevertheless, they are too fine to omit. (All three have restaurants open to the public. See pages 141 and 142.)

The Beekman Arms, Rhinebeck 12572. Phone: 876-7077. Rates: About $45 for a double, somewhat less from November to April. Reservations are essential and should be made well in advance. Credit cards accepted.

This inn, at the center of Rhinebeck on Route 9, lays claim

to being the oldest in continual operation in America. It was established in 1766, and guests have included everyone from George Washington and Aaron Burr (not at the same time) to Franklin D. Roosevelt and Nelson Rockefeller (also at different times).

Not much of the original structure remains, but at least it *looks* old. The exterior, with its white columns and greenhouse room for drinks, breakfast and lunch, is welcoming, and the interior public rooms, richly paneled, have the right feel for an old inn. But the rooms in this building are disappointing; small, not particularly attractive, even impersonal.

The very good news, though, is that the inn owns the Delameter House (see page 126), and this is where you should stay. It's very popular, so book well in advance. Operated as a Bed & Breakfast—the breakfast part is at the inn—you're left on your own in one of the absolutely delightful American Gothic rooms. (The Carriage House, completely modernized, is very comfortable and has its own pluses, but I much prefer staying in the main house.) This is the answer for a perfect location in Dutchess County near the Hudson and its many attractions.

Troutbeck, Amenia 12501. Phone: 373-8581. Rates: About $425 a couple, Friday night through Sunday lunch, including all meals and all spirits. Reservations required. Weekends only; during the week the inn is used as a conference center. Credit cards accepted.

The price is stiff and I, for one, don't like to be tied to one place for all my meals, but this is one of the more beautiful inns in the entire country, let alone the Valley. The original owner was a man named Joel Elias Spingarn, a most interesting individual. He was a founding member of the publishing firm of Harcourt, Brace as well as of the National Association for the Advancement of Colored People (NAACP), ran for Congress, wrote several books (including one on literary criticism in the Renaissance) and, last but not least, grew the largest collection of clematis in the world at Troutbeck. "It is the obsession of my leisure hours," he said.

Today the inn is set on 422 acres, with magnificient old sycamores in front, and elsewhere there are a lake and streams, a solar-heated pool, poolhouse, two tennis courts and walled gardens. All the accouterments, in short, of an estate, which is exactly what it is. To be more specific, an English country estate. The handsome stone Tudor house with leaded windows was built in 1919 and this is how architectural historian Lewis Mumford once described it: "Nestled under a hill, secure against even visual intrusion, [the] house cultivates its innerness; though numerous doors open onto lawn and terrace, Troutbeck itself gives a sense of being snug, protected, inviolate." At these prices, it should be. Sinclair Lewis liked it too, mentioning primarily the "cathedral of trees" around the building. In any case, the house has been impeccably restored and beautifully decorated, and you really will get your money's worth. (There's also an old farmhouse for guests, and if you're put there don't feel it's exile to Siberia. It, too, is perfection.)

Old Drover's Inn, Dover Plains 12522. Phone: 832-9311. Rates: About $55 for a double. Reserve well in advance. Closed Tuesday and Wednesday and for three weeks in December (so check beforehand if it's around the holidays). No credit cards accepted.

One small section of this lovely country inn goes back to about 1750, the rest was built by 1810, and of the three inns in Dutchess County this is my favorite. I suppose it's because I enjoy things on a small scale, but it also could be the fireplaces in the three bedrooms, or the murals in the Federal Room (particularly the one with an enormous urn filled with red tulips), or the taproom with paneling so dark it has an ebony glow, or the cheerful, yellow Meeting Room with its handsome barrel-vaulted ceiling. It could be all of these things, since together they add up to an ideal spot for a quiet country weekend.

Where to Eat

Three establishments in Dutchess County should get star billing.

The Culinary Institute of America (CIA), Hyde Park. Phone: 471-6608. On Route 9 between Hyde Park and Poughkeepsie. Credit cards accepted.

The CIA, as everyone calls it, is an enormous red-brick Geor-

gian colonial building that formerly was a seminary. (You'll see
the old chapel as you come up the drive.) Its purpose is to
educate around 1,850 students at a time in the culinary arts,
which it does well and thoroughly; chefs in good restaurants
across the country have graduated from here, and each gradua-
ting student will receive four or five job offers. Prominent
alumni include chefs at La Côte Basque in New York City, the
executive chef of the Royal Household in Jordan and the co-
owner of the Trellis in Colonial Williamsburg.

Two public dining rooms, *The Escoffier Room* and the *American Bounty Restaurant,* serve to display the burgeoning talents
of the students. (Saint Andrew's Cafe is also available to the
public for food, with the accent on good nutrition.) Both dining
rooms are extremely popular, not only because they can be
quite good and but also because they have received an enormous
amount of publicity. The result: You must reserve up to several
months in advance for a Friday or Saturday night. Don't go
there expecting one of the world's great meals. As the CIA itself
is careful to point out, these restaurants are "staffed by students
in the final course of the Institute's 21-month curriculum and
are intended to enhance their education. We say this not by way
of apology but as an explanation of why we especially appreciate your suggestions and understanding." A brilliantly put dis-
claimer, but it really isn't necessary.

Of the two restaurants my favorite is the American Bounty:
It's warm, inviting and informal. As you enter, for instance,
there's a cooking display window on your right, and under it are
wonderful, oversized wicker baskets packed to the brim with
fresh produce. There's always a selection of four or five freshly
baked breads, and these are served throughout dinner. The
wine list (American vintages only) is both outstanding and very
reasonably priced. And finally, of course, there's the food.

The menu changes daily and takes advantage of seasonal
produce. Sometimes the dishes can be too clever or even mediocre, but everything is prepared and presented with great style
and loving care, and sometimes, too, you can have something
that borders on great.

The Escoffier Room, as the name implies, is more of a classic
restaurant and thus deserves its more formal setting. There are
two rooms here; I prefer the one with the bar—a particularly

handsome one with stunning sconces—because it's more intimate than the main dining room and also because you can watch the students cooking. As to the food, the same praise and criticism applies as at the American Bounty. And once again, the wine list, this time more international in flavor, is excellent in both character and price.

The main thing, though, that makes dining at the CIA such a different and enjoyable experience is the students. They're wonderful. Serious and dedicated and trying so hard to please, they make you feel welcome and wanted and you find yourself rooting for their success as they tear about under the watchful eyes of faculty supervisors. (Does a dropped dish mean no A+? An overflowing ashtray banishment to the scullery?)

The dining rooms at the CIA serve dinner from 6:30 to 8:30 P.M. every day but Sunday and Monday. Closed on major holidays, the last week in June and the first week in July, and for two weeks at Christmas. Prices for entrées start at about $11 in the American Bounty. The Escoffier Room offers a prix-fixe dinner at about $30. Reservations required.

Harralds, Stormville. Phone: 878-6595. On Route 52. No credit cards accepted.

Harralds, a particularly attractive country inn set on well-tended grounds, is very much in the grand manner, featuring impeccable service, elegant food and fine wines (with prices to match). Sometimes the food can be a little too rich and a little too carefully thought out; one would like more straightforwardness and less sauce. Still, the quality of everything offered is first rate and the dishes are prepared and presented with consummate care. Portions are generous, too. Harrald himself is the host par excellence and makes sure that all goes flawlessly. I should also add that the restaurant has received several awards. There is a prix-fixe dinner of about $40. Open Wednesday–Friday, 6–9:30; Saturday sittings, 5:30 and 9:30; Sunday, 5–8:30. Closed Sunday from November to March and from January until mid-February. Reservations required.

Le Pavillon, Poughkeepsie. Phone: 473-2525. 230 Salt Point Turnpike. Credit cards accepted.

This is a real country French restaurant in a nice old house.

I like it for its good food and relaxed ambience. The chef-owner, Claude Guermont, a former chef-instructor at the CIA's Escoffier Room, was trained in France, but his food here is a combination of both French and American elements with a nouvelle cuisine bias. It is not, however, a bastion for nouvelle; Guermont uses the best of this, plus classical and regional cooking to create solidly based dishes with an original touch. The restaurant, oddly enough, never has a chicken dish on the menu, but game —pheasant, quail, partridge, venison—is always represented, as is a fresh fish of the day. Service is friendly, prices reasonable, and though the environs of Poughkeepsie may not be your idea of dinner in the country, you will be very happy here. Dinner served Monday–Saturday, 5:30–9:30; closed Sunday and all major holidays. Reservations required.

The remaining restaurants in Dutchess County range from adequate to good.

The Beekman Arms, Rhinebeck. Phone: 876-7077. On Route 9. Credit cards accepted. (See page 136.)

The dining rooms are crowded, the service friendly, the food, at best, moderately good American. Open for lunch and dinner. Lunch: 11:30–3. Sunday brunch: 10–2. Dinner: Monday–Friday, 5–10; Saturday, 5–11; Sunday, 3–10. Reservations usually needed, essential on weekends.

Old Drover's Inn, Dover Plains. Phone: 832-9311. Just off Route 22. No credit cards accepted. (See page 138.)

Good food—steaks, curries, an excellent pheasant roasted in wine, shrimp rarebit, etc.—in the perfect romantic setting. Expensive. Closed Tuesdays and Wednesdays and for three weeks in December. Lunch 12–3 on weekdays. Dinners: Monday, 5:30–8; Thursday, 5:30–9; Friday, 5:30–9:30; Saturday, 12–10; Sunday, 1–8:30. Reservations needed.

Schemmy's, Rhinebeck. Phone: 876-6215. Just off Route 9 at 19 East Market Street. No credit cards accepted.

An honest-to-God old-fashioned ice cream parlor and restaurant that serves a delicious breakfast (but no freshly squeezed orange juice), a good menu of sandwiches for lunch, and sundaes, shakes and splits from the fountain. Open seven days a week from 6 A.M. (Monday–Friday), 7 A.M. on Saturday and Sunday.

Troutbeck, Amenia. Phone: 373-8581. Credit cards accepted. (See page 137)

Dinner here consists of five courses and is good but not great —duck perfectly prepared, for example, marred by a slightly too sweet sauce—but the dining rooms are very pretty, the service friendly, and drinks from the open bar in one of the public rooms will make you think you are a private guest in a country house. A pleasant experience if not a gourmet's delight. Prix-fixe dinner about $30. Friday and Saturday nights only from 6:30–9:30; Saturday lunch, 12:30; Sunday brunch, 11–2:30. Reservations required.

THE
LOWER HUDSON
From Putnam County to
New York City

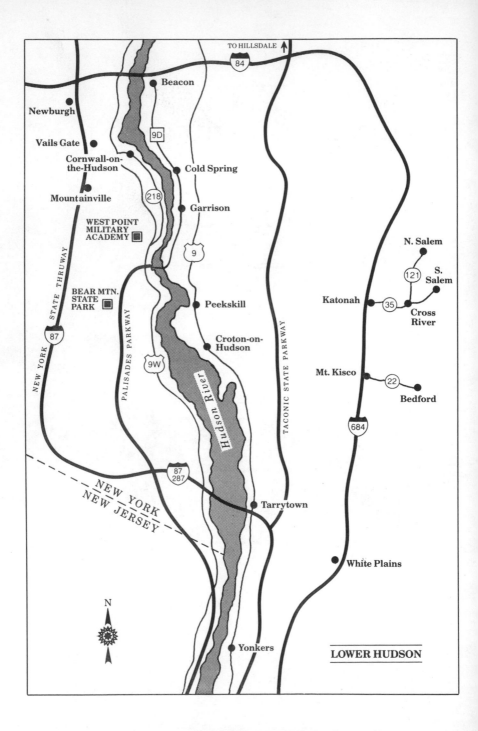

LOWER HUDSON

THIS is an area of near-violent contrasts: the most dramatic scenery on the River in the Highlands, the total ugliness of industrial concentration near New York City, the widest and narrowest points of the Hudson, the astounding beauty of the Palisades facing the grimy, falling-down piers, extreme wealth on baronial estates in Westchester County, dire poverty in dying urban centers such as Newburgh. Here you will enjoy museums and buildings and scenery of extraordinary interest and then, within only a few miles, come upon scenes of horrendous urban development.

The pace is different here, too; nervous energy radiates out from New York City, shattering the unity of the area into a vast urban-oriented, dependent complex that reflects, in a crazy-quilt way, the economy and vitality of the metropolis to the south. Sometimes the river seems to shrink to insignificance in the midst of it all, but don't be fooled. It is still the unifying link, an oasis of natural beauty that, no matter what man has tried to do, maintains its beauty and dignity. It just *is,* a great fact that moves on through it all, to its final destination far out in the Atlantic.

A Perfect Weekend in the Hudson Highlands

It sometimes happens when you arrive in a particular setting or place that you know this is it—here is the essence, good or bad, of the area you're exploring. In the Valley, that place is Cold Spring. Here and nearby can be found the most dramatic scenery not only on the Hudson but it must also rank among the most beautiful areas in the entire nation as well. The prettiest inn, some of the best restaurants, the most beautifully restored of all houses, West Point and Storm King, fine antique shops and excellent museums—plus a whole lot more. It is an ideal

place to spend a weekend, or longer, just absorbing this magnificently complex region, in terms both of nature and of history,
that constitutes the Hudson River Valley. What I describe
below would take more than a weekend, but you have the lux-
ury, then, of picking and choosing, and you can always come
back for more. You'll certainly want to.

THE SETTING

Cold Spring is in the Hudson Highlands, a 15-mile length of the
River that hasn't changed much since Henry Hudson first sailed
past in 1609. The highest mountains on the River are here,
rising straight up from the banks, and the Hudson reaches its
greatest depths here, as well. According to the most prevalent
geological theory, at this point the Hudson met another river
forcing its way north—all this many thousands of years ago—
and created the River we know today, where ocean tides sweep
as far north as Troy. Bordered on the north by Storm King and
on the south by Dunderberg Mountain, all the mountains
within this area are so steeply sloped that building development
is well-nigh impossible. What's more, today the region is protected further by the 52,000-acre Palisades Interstate Park and
the 16,000-acre United States Military Academy reservation at
West Point.

It is a stunning sight at any time of the year, but I particularly love it in the fall, the mountains ablaze with colors so
vibrant and alive they seem to flow down the sides to spread out
and shimmer on the blue palette of the River. One October,
when I was staying in Cold Spring for a few days to enjoy it all,
I would get up early each morning and look out my window to
see a thin luminous cloud hovering over the River, a silver
stripe dividing the reds and greens and golds and browns of the
mountains from the intense blue of the water. Slowly it would
rise and dissipate, a gauzy mystical curtain, and the Highlands
would appear, fully exposed in all their glory. It is the kind of
scenery that draws you into its very essence, making you forget
everything but the verity of those old clichés concerning water
and seasons, life and death, and—I have got to say it—truth and
beauty.

PUTNAM COUNTY

Cold Spring

Cold Spring is a small, pretty nineteenth-century village in Putnam County that does not, thank God, compete in any way with the surrounding scenery. On weekends it can be crowded, for Main Street is now packed with several dozen antique shops of varying quality that draw people like flies to honey. Still, you can spend a pleasant hour or two wandering through the different establishments; they carry everything and more—from furniture, paintings and prints to old pewter, china and glass to

Hudson House, the quintessential Hudson Valley inn, offers splendid views of the Highlands from the unspoiled setting of Cold Spring.

contemporary crafts, jewelry and "fabulous fifties" dreck. There is even one shop, "Mycroft Holmes," that has a small back room filled with memorabilia devoted to Mycroft's more famous brother Sherlock.

George Washington supposedly gave the town its name during the Revolution, but nothing much happened after that until the War of 1812, when President James Madison ordered a munitions foundry to be built here. It eventually constructed the nation's first iron ship and also the Parrott gun, a fieldpiece later used extensively in the Civil War. A man named Gouverneur Kemble (1786–1875) was appointed the foundry's first director, and it was he we also have to thank for the loveliest building in Cold Spring as well as one of the most charming in the entire Valley, the **Chapel of Our Lady**.

You reach the Chapel by going down Main Street toward the river. Turn left just before the railroad track (there's a sign there directing you to the Hudson House—more on that later) and then, once over the bridge covering the tracks, turn left again and, within a few feet, you will be at the back of the Chapel. Walk up the little steps and you are on a small bluff looking out across the river. Kemble donated both this site and the funds to build the Chapel, which was completed in 1833.

The building, small and simple, with a handsome front portico supported by four Doric columns, contains only one room. Thanks to the efforts of concerned citizens in the Valley, it has been perfectly restored. Originally a Catholic chapel, it is now an ecumenical church serving the entire community. (And more. Once, after I had mentioned the Chapel in an article for *Travel & Leisure* magazine, a young woman wrote me to say that she had traveled some distance to see the Chapel. She liked it so much, she told me, that she planned to be married there. That was nice to hear.)

The Chapel and view have always been a favorite of artists, but the most famous rendering of it—and certainly my favorite —is by William Henry Bartlett (1809–1854), an Englishman, whose rendition of the Chapel first appeared in London in 1840 in a book called *American Scenery* that became a classic of its time. In the latter half of the nineteenth century Bartlett's prints served as inspiration to such American painters as Thomas Chambers and Samuel Gerry as well as to countless folk artists. Bartlett's views of the Hudson, including this one, can still be found in antique and print shops at reasonable prices and make a wonderful memento of your time spent in the Valley. (In fact, if you go up Main Street, past the light and into Nelsonville, there, at 255 Main Street, you'll see Hudson Rogue Company. They offer a good, fairly priced selection of autographs, books and prints, including those of Bartlett. Phone: 914-265-2211.)

The Chapel is a favorite landmark of all those who sail the river, for it has a dignity and simplicity that is deeply moving. I remember that I first saw it one summer night, when it is softly floodlit, and it seemed so alone, somehow, not in a sad sense but so uniquely itself that nothing could touch it. Another time, on a dreary February day, I watched a wedding party being photographed there, under the handsome wrought-iron chandelier ablaze with red candles, and I thought how wonderful it would be to have the mileposts of one's life—births, marriages, deaths—recorded here in this Elysian setting that combines so brilliantly the best both man and nature have to offer.

When you leave, instead of turning back over the bridge, go straight to the end of the street, turn left and, at the end of the block on your right is **Hudson House**, the best inn in the Valley.

The first thing you'll notice is that you're right on the banks of the river, facing a small pier where steamboats used to dock and home to a little bandstand covered with a bright red roof. It's impossible, of course, not to walk out to the end of the pier before going into the inn, and once there you have still another spectacular view. To the south lies West Point, its chapel tower clearly visible against the sky. To the north, Storm King, somber and handsome, which Vincent J. Scully Jr., the famous architectural historian and author, termed "a dome of living granite, swelling with animal power. It is not picturesque in the softer sense of the word but awesome, a primitive embodiment of the energies of the earth. It makes the character of wild nature physically visible in monumental form." (The mountain was originally called Butter Hill, anathema to one Nathaniel Parker Willis [1806–1867], a now-forgotten writer-editor whose estate, "Idlewild," was in Cornwall on the west bank and who wrote the already-mentioned *American Scenery* that William

Bartlett illustrated. It was Willis who thought up the romantically descriptive Storm King and won the campaign to have this
become the mountain's official name.) By the way, usually there
are some swans here and a few ducks, so if you have any cookies
or crackers in your car, bring them along with you and make
some new, extremely greedy friends.

Now it's time to look more closely at the inn, a 3-story beige
clapboard structure with dormer windows, a bright blue door
and a porch running around the second floor. Built in 1832 to
house steamboat passengers, it was on its last legs in 1980 when
Mary Pat Sawyer bought it and, a million or so dollars later,
restored it—or, more accurately, created a delightful country
inn, many of whose rooms look directly out on the river. Each
guest room is furnished with country antiques and decorated
with individual flair. Very pleasant, and a welcome comfort to
the traveler.

Downstairs, three of the small, papered dining rooms with
comfortable, painted Windsor chairs face the river, and don't be
afraid to kill to get a window table. On the street side is the
small bar and long, nicely furnished lounge, with a roaring
fireplace in winter and where guests also eat when the dining
rooms are full. (There is also a garden for summer dining.)
These rooms have flowered cotton prints at the windows and
comfortable chairs for diners and loungers. Service is friendly
and informal, and as a place to stay there is little that could be
faulted. As for the food, it's good enough but could be better. The
menu is basically American and offers a smallish selection
that's reasonably well prepared and priced but hardly exciting.
I would certainly stay over and eat here one night, for the view
and the pleasant ambience; for the same reason I'd definitely
recommend dining here once even if you can't stay over but
want a special place on the river for at least one meal.

For one of your weekend nights, though, I strongly suggest
that you eat at **Plumbush**, a particular favorite of mine. The
food is excellent, the dining room inviting and the service superb—all at a reasonable price. Go back up Main Street to
Route 9D, turn right, and you'll see a sign for the restaurant on
your left after you've driven a mile or so. Owned by two Swiss,
Gieri Albin, the host, and Ans Benderer, the chef, Plumbush is
in an old, rambling barn of a house once owned by a woman with

the grand-sounding name of Marchesa Rizzo dei Ritii; her maiden name was plain old Agnes Shewan.

The dining rooms, in various shapes and sizes, are either papered or paneled in dark oak and hung with (mostly) attractive art, much of which is for sale. Each has its own wood-burning fireplace, a particular delight for a fire freak like me, and there is the usual candlelight at each table.

The menu is primarily continental with Swiss overtones. The food is excellent and prepared with great care. I have never had a disappointing meal here, but I particularly favor a squab chicken stuffed with wild rice and served with an orange-and-chutney sauce, or the medallions of pork with chestnuts and apples Bernoise. My favorite dish of all, though, is a dessert, Swiss apple fritters, crisp and delicious and served with a sauce that perfectly complements the apples. The wine list is more than adequate and, like the food, fairly priced. This is one of the more pleasant places to dine along the Hudson.

What to See and Do

Boscobel Literally a stone's throw beyond Plumbush is the entrance to Boscobel, an architecturally magnificent building that, of all the Hudson River houses, has the most spectacular interior. Overall, it is the finest example I know of the New York Federal period (roughly 1780–1820) in terms of architecture, furniture and decoration. And, certainly, Federal was one of the most elegant styles in our history.

Placed high over the river, with views extending for miles, the exterior of Boscobel glows in its original colors—a creamy white for the trim, yellow ochre for the walls. It resembles an airy, elegant stage set, with the blue-gray Hudson an ever-present motif. This feeling is reinforced by the carved wooden swags between the columns that set off the balcony on the second floor. Surrounding the mansion is a landscape of lawns, woods, gardens and orchards.

The house was the dream of States Morris Dyckman, a descendant of early Dutch settlers, who was born in New York City in 1775. A Loyalist during the Revolution, Dyckman went to London for the duration, returning to this country in 1789. In 1804, he and his wife, Elizabeth, began planning the country

The orangerie at Boscobel. The house and setting are among the most beautiful in the country, the restoration a triumph of research and taste.

estate they decided to call Boscobel, both because *bosco bello* meant "beautiful woods" in Italian and also in memory of the Shropshire forest where Charles II hid himself inside an oak tree after being defeated by Cromwell at the battle of Worcester in 1651.

But Dyckman died in 1806, before the house was completed (the architect, by the way, is unknown), and it was left to Elizabeth to finish. Boscobel remained in the family until 1888, then fell on hard times. By 1954 demolition seemed inevitable; in 1955, a check for $35 bought the house, and plans were made to tear it down. Like all good stories, though, this one has a happy ending. The house was saved, moved to its present site, a few miles further north, and rebuilt, primarily through the generosity of Lila Acheson Wallace, co-founder with her husband De Witt of *Reader's Digest*. Boscobel Restoration, a nonprofit group, was set up to handle the refurbishing of the mansion, and in 1961, it was opened to the public. Then, in 1975, a copy of a list of States Dyckman's possessions was found that indicated the furnishings were quite different from what the house now contained. Mrs. Wallace again came to the rescue; the offending collection was sold and, within two years, the New York Federal furniture you presently see put in its place.

Once through the front door, you enter the great hall, which faces a magnificent central staircase that rises to a landing with a huge Palladian window. The staircase divides to the left and right and continues to the second floor. Doric columns support three arches that separate the hall into two sections. The overall style is that of Robert Adam, the Scottish architect and designer who had an enormous influence in this country during the late eighteenth and nineteenth centuries.

Because the hall's architecture is so beautiful, the restorers decided that the decoration should emphasize its detail. A wallpaper was found in the 1804 Medford Inn in Massachusetts and reproduced for Boscobel. The pattern resembles carved stonework in tan and buff, and the doors, columns and trim are painted in the original ivory color. (Here, as elsewhere in the house, the original colors were found through microscopic examination of the cracks and crevices where the early paint still remained.) The floor of the great hall is covered with a floor cloth—very similar to our linoleum—that has been handpainted to look like marble and is based on a pattern found in a book published in the late eighteenth century.

To the right of the hall are the parlors. In the front one, most of the furniture is by, or attributed to, Duncan Phyfe, the great New York cabinetmaker, and the chairs and sofa are covered in a brilliant lemon-yellow moreen upholstery. There are other Phyfe pieces throughout the house, making it almost a museum of his work.

A portrait of Elizabeth Dyckman—feminine and pretty, although rumor has it that she was tight with a dollar—hangs over the sofa, and the draperies are reproduced from period ones found in the attic of another Hudson Valley home. And here, as almost everywhere in the house, fresh flowers in Chinese export bowls give the impression that the owners have stepped out only for a moment, leaving instructions that their visitors be made to feel at home. Behind this room is a second parlor that includes part of States Dyckman's library.

Recross the hall and you enter the most beautiful part of the house, the dining room. The proportions are ideal, the carving of the architectural detail that of a master craftsman, the colors warm, soft and inviting. The design of the mantelpiece, as for those in the parlors, is similar to plans in William Payne's *The Gentleman and Country Builder's Companion* (1794). The dining-room table is spectacular—in three parts, with the center section in front of the window facing the Hudson. It can seat 24 when put together, but in its present, reduced state it is set for 6, with some original pieces including Elizabeth's monogrammed silver.

Two Federal sideboards, early and late period, stand against the walls, and the chairs, their backs and legs carved to imitate bamboo and painted a soft cream with green trim, are similar to the ones Elizabeth Dyckman had bought in New York. The whole feeling of the room—straight lines offset by graceful curves, symmetrical outlines, even fragile construction—is one of repose. In a small pantry behind the dining room are cupboards filled with blue-and-white porcelain.

On either side of the staircase landing, there are pictures of Elizabeth's great-grandparents, done in 1726 by portraitist John Watson. At the head of the stairs is a painting of Narcissus by Benjamin West. To the left are a guest bedroom, a dressing room and Elizabeth Dyckman's own room. Hers, of course, is the most beautiful, with its Phyfe canopy bed, needlepoint rug and portraits of her husband and son.

The central part of the upstairs is taken up by an enormous library-sitting room whose floor-length windows open onto the balcony. Two of Boscobel's most beautiful pieces of furniture are here: a bookcase with desk, again attributed to Phyfe, with the arms of Thomas Witter Chrystie, a New York attorney, the first-known example of any New York furniture bearing a coat of arms; and an octagonal card table covered in green baize and leather, which was found lying in pieces against a furnace in the nearby village of Cold Spring. The other two rooms on this floor are a bath and nursery, the latter complete even down to a cradle of the period.

The basement once consisted of a root cellar and two kitchens. Now it is devoted primarily to exhibition space. In a way, this is the heart of the house, for here you find the original material that set the tone for the restoration. There are family documents and the china, glass and silver purchased by States Dyckman in England; a medallion carved from a piece of the Royal Oak in the forest of Boscobel in England; even examples of china with companion bills alongside describing the English country scenes painted on them. Look, also, for two pairs of portraits of Hudson Valley gentry, one pair by Ammi Phillips, the other by Ralph Earl; they are masterpieces of their kind. You exit out into the grounds through the restored kitchen, warm and comfortable with Hudson Valley chairs and tools of the time.

Boscobel is set on 45 acres of land, about 15 of which are landscaped. In the spring, 2,8000 tulips and flowering fruit trees greet the visitor. In summer a formal rose garden scents the air, and geraniums and begonias stand out vividly against the greenness of lawn and surrounding woods. All the grounds are open to the public.

There is also a well-stocked gift shop with everything from candles and soap to jams and jellies, from 10-cent candy sticks to reproduction china. In the fall, you can buy apples picked from the trees on the estate, and in winter a fire always burns both in the shop and in the kitchen of the mansion.

As you leave, look back. Your view is framed by the alley of hemlock hedges . . . and there, at the other end, is one last view of the Hudson, now silver in the reflected light.

Boscobel is open daily except Tuesday, April–October, 9:30–5. In March, November and December, 9:30–4. Closed January and February, Thanksgiving and Christmas day. Admission: $4.00; children, $2.00. Phone: 914-265-3638.

ORANGE COUNTY

West Point

West Point is within easy driving distance of Cold Spring. Go south on Route 9D to the Bear Mountain Bridge, cross the Hudson into Orange County, and then go north on 9W, following the West Point signs and eventually getting on Route 218N, which will take you right to the grounds of the Academy. Stop first at the Information Center, open daily 9:30–4:30, except Thanksgiving, Christmas, and New Year's Day, where you can look at displays and films concerning the Academy and also pick up informational literature. Be sure to include a map of the grounds, vital to your getting around easily.

HISTORY

With the onset of the Revolution, it became immediately apparent that the Hudson would have to be secured against the British. For one thing, it was the natural invasion route from Canada and, for another, if it ever fell under British control, that meant New England would be cut off from the rest of the colonies. Congress appointed a committee under George Washington to study the matter and they quickly concluded that the best stronghold was in the Highlands. Here it was easiest to protect the water corridor and, in addition, this was also where the major northeast-to-southwest land routes lay that could be used by the American Army to move supplies and men between New England and the Middle Atlantic colonies.

This all happened in 1775. By 1777, because of bickering, stalling and general inertia—plus the appointment of a Dutch botanist with almost nothing to recommend him to the post of military engineer—very little had been done. The Hudson still lay open to the British. That same year General Burgoyne did, in fact, come down from Canada (see page 19). In late summer General Sir Henry Clinton sent a message to Burgoyne that he would be moving north to assist him. It was already too late. The message reached Burgoyne on September 21, 1777, just after the first part of the Saratoga campaign had ended so badly for him and his men.

On October 3 Clinton began his move, and by October 6 he had defeated the American forces in the Highlands. The River was now open all the way to Albany, and the elated British proceeded farther north to burn Kingston (see page 86) and Clermont (see page 52). That's when they got the news that Burgoyne had been forced to surrender. Clinton's troops fell back to New York City, leaving the Hudson safe once more in American hands.

Even after that, the Americans didn't learn their lesson. They dithered about until 1778 when they finally got together and decided that West Point should be fortified and occupied as a post. It has never been unoccupied since. Things looked even better after the appointment of Colonel Tadeusz Kosciuszko, a French-trained Polish army officer, as chief engineer, and he began fortifying the entire surrounding area as well—work that continued far into the next year. By the time Kosciuszko was finished, the Americans had a fortified area greatly ahead of its time: several mutually strong points along the river instead of one fortified position as had been the rule since the eighteenth century.

It was in 1778, too, that the Great Chain between West Point and Constitution Island was put in place to prevent British ships from sailing up the Hudson. The chain was a major undertaking for its time. The iron came from New Jersey and the lower Catskills. The forged links were taken north of West Point, joined together to form the chain, and then fastened to logs that served as floats. These carried the chain downstream to the points on both shores where it was to be anchored by huge blocks of wood and stone. (An earlier chain between Fort Montgomery and Anthony's Nose had been put in place in 1776, but it soon broke. As for this one, no enemy ship ever came this far upriver after 1778 to test its effectiveness.)

The next—and last—real threat to the security of West Point was the treason of Benedict Arnold. After his inspired actions at Saratoga (see page 21), the height of his glory, Arnold's career slid slowly downhill. Posted to Philadelphia, he did so poorly that he was reprimanded by Washington and even faced a court-martial. The one bright light for him was Peggy Shippen, the ravishingly beautiful eighteen-year-old daughter of a Tory sympathizer, whom he married in 1779. No one seems to know exactly what role Peggy, who came from a prominent Philadelphia family, played in Arnold's eventual betrayal, but it was around this time that he made contact with Captain John André, aide to General Clinton, and offered his services to the Crown.

Clinton soon let Arnold know what he wanted—West Point. And, for $20,000, Arnold said he would deliver it up. It was at this stage that Washington decided to utilize Arnold as an auxiliary commander of his left flank in an attack on New York City.

Arnold begged off, asking for command of West Point instead. For some reason, Washington relented and gave it to him.

On September 21, 1780, André sailed up the Hudson on HMS *Vulture*—the same ship, incidentally, that had been used by the squadron sent to burn Kingston and the Livingston estate at Clermont—and met Arnold on shore south of Verplanck's Point. Unfortunately for André, the Americans (under Colonel James Livingston, appropriately enough) began shelling the *Vulture,* forcing the ship to retreat southward. André was left stranded (literally high and dry, you might say). On his way back to rejoin the British lines he was captured, tried and hanged as a spy. Arnold himself narrowly escaped being caught, but went on to serve in the English army as a brigadier general, leading troops in both Virginia and Connecticut. In 1781, Arnold left the colonies for England where he and Peggy lived in disgrace and poverty until his death in 1801.

After these events the war shifted elsewhere and although Washington and others had strongly urged the founding of a national military academy to provide professional officers—it "has ever been considered by me as an object of primary importance to this country," Washington pleaded—it wasn't until 1802, under President Thomas Jefferson, that legislation established the United States Military Academy at West Point. The Academy first opened its doors that same year, on Independence Day, with 10 cadets. Today there are almost 4,500 men and women at the Academy, and its graduates have dominated the leadership of all our wars from the Civil (both Grant and Lee) to the present. (It is sobering to realize that in the War Between the States, of the 60 major battles, 55 were commanded on *both* sides by West Point graduates.)

The Academy Grounds   Your first stop should be at the **West Point Museum** in Thayer Hall. The collection was started in 1777, after the Battle of Saratoga, when British weaponry was sent here. The Museum opened to the public in 1854, and today it houses more military relics than any other such edifice in the western hemisphere. The collection could be boring—how many guns, uniforms and swords do you really need to see?—but it has been arranged so imaginatively that it becomes a fascinating experience.

The first room, for instance, sometimes has on display a wonderful detailed model of the *Mary Powell*, the nineteenth-century steamboat that was known as "the Queen of the Hudson" and is generally acknowledged to be the most beautiful ever to ply its waters. And there is more than just American history; excellent dioramas depict major battles from Cynoscephalae (197 B.C.) to Gettysburg (1863). There are, of course, the historical memorabilia (uniforms belonging to Grant, Patton and Eisenhower; an Indian painting of Custer's "Last Stand"; some sinister Nazi paraphernalia including Göring's handgun; astronaut Frank Borman's pressurized space suit) but there are also such oddities as historical musical instruments and some of the links from the iron chain that stretched from West Point across to Constitution Island.

Among my own favorite exhibits are the full-scale replicas of military life that range from a nineteenth-century frontier stockade to a portion of a trench in World War I; the stunning 3,000-figure collection of exquisitely made soldiers representing the ensemble of troops that constituted Napoleon's Grande Armée; the flags and posters that are everywhere; the gallery devoted to the American Revolution. My favorite single object: A Civil War painting that, with a little too much sentimentality but in all sincerity, shows the family tragedy of war. Titled

Fat and sassy, the pleasure boat Commander *chugs by the looming gray walls of West Point, which seem faintly disapproving of the intrusion.*

Spirit of xmas eve '62, the main portion of the canvas contains two large medallions surrounded by evergreens. In one a mother is praying at a window, her children asleep nearby. The other portrays the uniformed father, in the woods, gazing at a picture of his family. In the upper left corner, Santa Claus makes an appearance on the rooftop, while in the upper right an army camp stands in bleak contrast. In the lower left corner soldiers are mending their uniforms in the snow, while in the lower right a ship sinks in a violent storm. Flags and tombstones fill the rest of the canvas. A curious work, yet strangely effective, even haunting, in its expression of genuine feeling.

My least favorite object is downstairs. There, among military weapons, swords, pistols, artillery arms and armor is the case of the atomic bomb developed during the Manhattan Project (1943–45) and first used over Nagasaki. Its nicknames were "Fat Man" and "The Little Boy," light-hearted euphemisms for such a ghastly instrument. The casing is obscenely ugly. Brown and stubby, it looks like some hideous magnified abstraction of a nightmarish insect, and its image stays too long in the mind. (The Museum is open daily, 10:30–4:15 except January 1 and Christmas day. Admission: Free.)

From the Museum go next to **the most famous view on the Hudson**, just off Washington Road at the northernmost point and by the monument to Major General John Sedgwick, killed at Spotsylvania in the Civil War's Wilderness campaign. You've seen it a million times in movies and photographs (usually, it seems to me, with some cadet annoyingly in the foreground, his back turned to the camera), but it remains a thrill, nonetheless, viewed "live": the great river coming down right through the Highlands and the Catskills a hazy blue in the far distance. In combination with the surrounding monuments, particularly the nearby Battle Monument inscribed with the names of 2,230 men killed in the Civil War, it is guaranteed to bring out the most latent feelings of patriotism.

Your next stop should be the **Cadet Chapel (1910)**, for me a curiously unsuccessful building. The architect was Bertram Grosvenor Goodhue (1869–1924) of the firm Cram, Goodhue & Ferguson, who designed a number of other buildings at West Point. My favorite work of the theirs, though, is in New York City—St. Thomas' Episcopal Church (1914) which, like the

Chapel here, is also a Gothic building. During the first three decades of this century Cram, Goodhue & Ferguson were considered the country's foremost church architects and primary exponents of the Gothic style. Goodhue himself also designed St. Bartholomew's Episcopal Church (1919) in New York, the Los Angeles Public Library (1924) and, considered to be his masterpiece, the Nebraska State Capitol (1928) in Lincoln.

There's no denying that this chapel has a handsome exterior, and its spectacular location high above the campus adds to its sense of dominance. In fact, it's most beautiful when seen from afar ("distance lends enchantment . . ."). Yet it is cold, even to the point of sterility. Is it the forbidding battlements and crenellated towers? Or could it be the strangely lifeless gray of the West Point granite from which it is built? Gothic should be soaring and elevating, but this building doesn't soar, it looms. You feel almost unwelcome approaching it.

The interior, thankfully, is less forbidding, and here the verticality of the architecture does indeed soar. The first thing you notice are the battle flags that go back to the Civil War hanging from the triforium. They add a dignified military touch to the whole. Then there is the stained glass, all of which was designed by William and Anne Lee Willet of the Stained Glass and Decorating Company in Philadelphia. Not terribly good, I think. But what makes the interior seem so austere are the stone floors and arches and the brown brick walls and surface between the ribs of the vaults—not to mention some particularly ugly lights on the side walls and below the triforium made of opaque glass and using fluorescent bulbs. Taken all in all, there is, admittedly, a very real sense of dignity to the place, and I suppose many would consider this interior to be on a scale that might be termed awesome. For me, though, I find it devoid of humanity. (Open: Daily, 8–4:15. Admission: Free.)

Far more interesting, I'd say, is the lovely **Old Cadet Chapel** (**1836**) that stands at the entrance to West Point's cemetery. Greek Revival in style, with four white Doric columns, the exterior has a quiet, simple elegance that is most effective. Inside, white Ionic columns support the curved ceiling, nicely setting off the plain wooden floor and carpeting and the pews with their handsome wooden armrests, while the clear glass windows, wide and rounded at the top, let the light flood in. There's an unpretentious, even virile dignity here that I miss in the new chapel. At the front, behind and above a red velvet screen topped by a gilded eagle with spread wings, is a mural representing War (a Roman soldier) and Peace (a young woman—dressed in white, naturally).

Far more moving, though, are the simple black marble plaques with their gold lettering dedicated to early American officers that cover the walls between the windows and also the handsome old cannons, embedded in those same walls, snub snouts pointed at the ceiling. For me this chapel sums up and symbolizes the values and traditions of West Point better than anything else on the grounds, and gives a special, even unique, insight into the history and meaning of the Academy. (Open: Daily, 8–4:15. Admission: Free.)

A River Cruise on the Commander

If, when you enter the gates at West Point, you turn right at the first divide in the road, you will come down to the river and to a pleasant little park with picnic tables scattered about along the bank. It is from here that you can board the *Commander* for a scenic cruise either to the north into the Highlands or south past the Bear Mountain Bridge, depending on which route you choose. The boat looks more like a jolly toy than a real operating vessel, with its brightly colored awning over the top deck and its chubby outline, and it puts you into an appropriately festive mood. The last time I enjoyed her hospitality we left about 2 P.M. and cruised down toward the Bear Mountain Bridge. Because it was toward the end of the season, a crystal clear and brilliant September day, not many people were aboard, and even fewer were on the exposed top deck to enjoy the autumn colors and the passing river landscape.

It was as we were going under the bridge itself that I was told a marvelous story of how the bridge came to be built. It seems that Mrs. E. H. Harriman, wife of the railroad tycoon and mother of former United States Ambassador and New York State Governor Averell Harriman, found it highly inconvenient to go from her estate on the west bank to visit her friends on the east bank, so she decided to build a bridge to solve her

problem. Friends and advisers all told her she was a fool—
politely, of course—but Mrs. Harriman smilingly ignored them
and forged ahead, not at all daunted, spending a rumored $5
million to create her "little time-saver," which also turned out
to be the longest suspension bridge in the world. When it was
finished, she promptly put a toll booth at the western entrance;
in 1940, when the bridge was sold to New York State, the proceeds plus the tolls netted the Harrimans a nice little bundle.
I don't know if the details are true—I hope so—but it certainly
is true that the Harrimans built this lovely suspension bridge
rising 185 feet above the Hudson.

In any case, do take the *Commander.* The next time I'd like
to go upriver; I've watched her pass by at dusk, lights ablaze,
from Cold Spring. At the same time, it would be a fine opportunity to see Bannerman's Island, one of the more romantic spots
in the Hudson. Francis Bannerman was a dealer in U.S. Army
and Navy surplus equipment who bought up most of the weapons captured in the Spanish-American War. The perfect place
to store them, he decided, would be on this island, which he
promptly purchased and named after himself. He dredged out
a small harbor and built turreted walls around it. Then he
erected a Scottish castle for his summer home and an arsenal
for the weapons and settled back to enjoy life. Today the island
is owned by New York State and is a part of the Hudson Highlands State Park. It's dangerous to go ashore because the buildings are in such an advanced state of decay, but that doesn't
seem to deter most people. Seen from the deck of a boat as it
cruises past, it must be a wonderful sight, this rugged, romantic
ruin just north of Storm King.

The *Commander* is operated by Hudson Highlands Cruises
and Tours, Inc., in Highland Falls. Phone: 914-446-7171. It operates from May to October, with several cruises each day leaving
from West Haverstraw and West Point. Call in advance for
reservations.

Storm King Mountain

When you are ready to leave West Point, follow the main road
north and, as you exit the grounds, turn right on 218, here a

narrow, winding, two-lane country road that passes through woods, then rises and takes you along Storm King and to a breathtaking view of the Highlands. There are several places along the way where you can pull your car off the road to enjoy the view, but by far the best is a tiny spot, big enough for only a car or two and at the highest spot on the drive. From here the River can be seen at its most majestic as it passes between the mountains. Trains on the opposite bank are toys, cars seem as small as ladybugs, a seaplane passes below you, pleasure boats become whitecaps on the swelling flow. But what you are most aware of is the wind, the River and the utter tranquillity of the scene at your feet.

It was here that, back in the 1960's, Consolidated Edison of New York decided to build a power plant, the largest of its kind in the world—it could have drawn six *billion* gallons of river water each day into its storage reservoir—at the base of the mountain. Fortunately, it was one of those proposals that galvanize people into action, and up and down the Hudson residents rose in wrath. Con Ed eventually backed down, thus ensuring —forever, one hopes—that the mountain remains an undisturbed natural treasure for all to enjoy.

A Very Special Museum in Orange County

The Museum of the Hudson Highlands   Continue north, descending the mountain, and soon you'll see, as you approach Cornwall, a sign for the Museum of the Hudson Highlands. For several years I had wondered what this could be all about but never made the effort to find out. Finally one afternoon, with some extra time on my hands, I decided to drop in. What I discovered was an ideal spot for children and a wonderfully endearing little museum for adults. I urge you to go there.

The museum's purpose is to study the natural and cultural history of the Hudson Valley, and it's located in a handsome, rustic stone-and-wood building that is surrounded by a forest. There's even a stream flowing beneath the galleries; a more charming setting would be hard to find. Set up in 1959 specifically to provide children with educational and recreational programs unavailable locally, the museum now engages in other activities as well, such as Project SOAR, a major effort to restore the populations of the bald eagle, osprey and peregrine falcon in the Valley.

But that's enough background; on to the exhibits! The Natural History Wing is my favorite, for here are the live animals, birds, reptiles and fish that make it so much fun. What's more, all are native to the Hudson. I really like the owls, they always look so silly, but my favorite is Crowbar, a crow who screeches "Hello!" periodically but doesn't look like he really means it. There's even an Indian wigwam. Needless to say, kids go wild here and have to be dragged away.

I wasn't in any rush to leave myself, but when I did I discovered that there are self-guiding nature trails through 70 acres of mature forest. I wasn't quite ready to explore it all, but I walked enough of it to know that I'd like to come back, perhaps with a picnic on some perfect summer day. And, anyway, I want to see Crowbar do his routine again.

The museum is open Saturday—Thursday. Closed Friday. Summer hours: 11–5 weekdays, 12–5 weekends. Winter hours:

One of the manifold pleasures of back roads is coming upon dignified, well-designed old homes like this one nestled deep in the country.

2–5 weekdays, 12–5 Saturday, 1:30–5 Sunday. Admission: Donation. Phone: 914-534-7781.

Newburgh

If you continue on Route 218 you will soon come to Route 9W.
Take it north to Newburgh. This is one of the saddest sites on
the Hudson, for the once lovely river town was largely destroyed by an urban renewal program that tore down but did
nothing else. It could have happened in Kingston, too, except
that men like Fred Johnston (see page 86) stopped it and, instead, restored what they had. Newburgh had no such luck.
(There is some good news, though; people are beginning to move
there and buy up some of the older houses at bargain-basement
prices. But even with all this restoration, it will be a long, hard
struggle to bring the city back.) In any case, the reason I suggest
coming to Newburgh is that three locations closely associated
with the American Revolution are here or nearby, as is Storm
King Art Center.

Washington's Headquarters,   84 Liberty St. Open: April–
December, Wednesday–Saturday 10–5, Sunday 1–5. Closed Jan-
uary 1, Thanksgiving and Christmas day. Admission: Free.
Phone: 914-562-1195 for hours open January–March.

After the Battle of Yorktown in 1781, it was still necessary to
keep the Continental Army together until the negotiations
leading up to the Treaty of Paris—which formally acknowledged the independence of the United States—could be completed. Therefore, the army remained encamped at nearby New
Windsor while, from April 1782 to August 1783, Washington
took up residence in this house, which then belonged to members of Jonathan Hasbrouck's family. (Hasbrouck, a successful
farmer and merchant, served in the military as a colonel but
was forced to retire in 1778 because of ill health. He died in
1780.) The house descended through the family until 1850, when
New York State bought it to preserve as a historic site.

You first enter an adjacent museum that is, in many ways,
more interesting than the house itself. There's an excellent
slide presentation here and, even better, the permanent exhibits contain much interesting memorabilia relating to the Revo-

lution. Then, when you are through, a guide will take you to the house with its view across the Hudson to the east bank. The building is tiny, and it's hard to imagine it as the headquarters for the general of a victorious army. When the Marquis de Chastellux, who had fought with Washington during the Revolution, came here to bid his final farewell before returning to France, he noted that only one room was "tolerably spacious" and that even that one was broken up by seven doors and one window. He was wrong; there are eight doors in this room, the first that you will visit.

There are eight rooms in all and the tour is well-conducted and generally informative. Outside again, take a look at the rather startling "Tower of Victory," a monument put up on the centennial of the signing of the Treaty of Paris, which Washington learned about in this house.

Knox Headquarters, Forge Hill Road, Vails Gate. Open: Wednesday-Saturday 9–5, Sunday 1–5. Closed: January 1, Thanksgiving and Christmas day. Admission: Free. Phone: 914-561-5498.

This is a pretty Georgian house, only about 3 miles from Washington's headquarters, and frankly it is more interesting for its period charm than for its rather minimal historical import. It was built by Thomas Ellison who had settled in the area in the 1720's and prospered, erecting this house in 1754 for his son, John. By the time the Revolution rolled around, John, too, was doing very well, thanks to a nearby grist mill from which he sent his flour in his own sloops down to the family wharves in New York City.

During the War two other generals aside from Knox stayed here, Nathanael Greene and Horatio Gates, but it is Henry Knox, a close friend and adviser to Washington, who is most closely associated with the house and wrote his wife happily from here that he had a "very good Bedchamber in a warm Stone House." The place remained in the Ellison family until 1891. In 1918 the Knox Headquarters Association bought it and transferred ownership to New York State four years later.

New Windsor Cantonment, Temple Road, Vails Gate. Open: Mid-April to October, Wednesday–Saturday 10–5, Sunday 1–5. Admission: Free. Phone: 914-561-1765.

It was here, during 1782 and '83, that the Continental Army
of about 8,000 officers and enlisted men encamped in the most
substantial quarters of the Revolution while awaiting news
from Paris about the final peace.

The original cantonment covered a two-and-a-half-square-
mile area and contained some 700 log cabins laid out in rows
along the linear patterns the army would follow in case of battle. Wood came from the nearby forests and the huts were built
by the 16 soldiers assigned to each.

When the housing and other essential buildings were completed, a chaplain suggested that a large hall be constructed for
religious services and public assemblies. Up it went and was
named the Temple of Virtue. It was in the Temple that Washington addressed his officers and narrowly averted a mutiny
arising from the affair of the Newburgh Letters, in which his
officers were urged to rebel and force Congress to meet their
demands for back pay and pensions. The cantonment was also
the site where Washington named the first soldier to receive the
Badge of Military Merit, a decoration that would later become
the Purple Heart.

After the war formally ended, the soldiers drifted back to
their homes and the buildings were auctioned off, dismantled
and taken away to disappear from history—except for one,
which was bought by a man named Sackett. He added it to his
house, where it remained until restored to its original site in
1934. It is the only original building in the cantonment.

Today the site contains reconstructed buildings, special exhibits, reenactments of the Revolutionary soldier's life, and
army-crafts displays. Uniformed staff members also demonstrate weapons and present military drills daily.

Storm King Art Center, Old Pleasant Hill Road, Mountain-
ville. Open: Mid-May to October, daily 2–5:30. Closed Tuesday.
Admission: $2. Phone: 914-534-3115.

The setting for this open-air major center of contemporary
sculpture placed decoratively about the grounds is 200 acres of
magnificent land that includes landscaped gardens, fields and
lawns. You approach the museum along a driveway bordered by
trees, through which you can already see some examples from
the permanent collection of more than 200 sculptures, the work

All that is left of Danskammer House are these columns moved to Storm King Art Center and still regal in their lonely splendor.

of such artists as David Smith (13 examples of his work alone), Isamu Noguchi, Alexander Calder, Henry Moore, Barbara Hepworth, and Louise Nevelson.

The museum was originally built in the French-Norman style as a residence for Vermont Hatch, a New York City lawyer, out of stones he had bought from the just-demolished Danskammer House, a famous Greek Revival residence just north of Newburgh.

Danskammer had been built in 1834 by Edward Armstrong, the son of a British officer who, although he'd fought against the patriots in the Revolution, nevertheless decided to stay in the United States after the war. The house was so beautiful that many people tried to save it from being razed, but they failed, unfortunately. In 1935 Mr. Hatch took the remains, including the splendid Ionic columns, to form his new residence. The columns have been preserved and now stand just south of the museum on a lovely spot high above the gently rolling fields.

Each year the museum offers changing exhibits of prominent American and European artists to enhance its permanent collection. Frankly, whether you are interested in contemporary sculpture or not, the setting is so pleasant that you could go there just to enjoy the views and explore the landscape.

WESTCHESTER COUNTY

Other Special Places in the Lower Hudson Valley

Caramoor Museum, Katonah. Open: April–November, Wednesday–Saturday 10–4, Sunday 1–4. Admission: $4. Phone: 914-232-5035.

I first discovered Caramoor through the summer music festival held there in July and August, an event that takes place on the grounds of this grand estate either in the Venetian Theater, an exquisite outdoor site whose stage is framed by an arcade of (logically enough) Venetian columns, or in the Spanish Courtyard, part of the house itself.

The Spanish-style house was built by Walter Rosen (1875–1951), a New York lawyer, and his wife, Lucie Dodge, in the 1930's following the designs of Mr. Rosen. I find it a curious, intensely personal building; artistic treasures rest cheek by jowl with things that definitely aren't, but the overall impression is, no doubt about it, one of magnificence.

The tour takes you through the rooms on the first floor. The most striking, I'd say, is the seventeenth-century painted Library that was brought over in its entirety from France and incorporated into the house, as were several of the other rooms. What one immediately notices is the glorious blue of the background, particularly on the ceiling. I've never seen its like anywhere, and it's startlingly lovely. The groin-vaulted ceiling is filled with biblical scenes in amazing colors, and the door panels are painted, too. It's an enchanting room, one you will want to linger in.

By far the most dramatic room is the immense Music Room, which extends the full length of the north wing of the house. High, wide and handsome, it has, for instance, a sixteenth-century carved wood coffered ceiling designed in squares and crosses with center rosettes that was shipped to Caramoor from a palazzo in southern Italy. But this room holds all kinds of surprises: sixteenth-century stained glass from France and

Switzerland, a seventeenth-century Turkish rug, eighteenth-century Italian armchairs, a bride's chest from Spain, ruby velvet sixteenth-century Italian curtains, a terra-cotta relief from the workshops of Andrea della Robbia. Eclectic, yes, and some of the pieces and art works I could do without, but definitely sumptuous and even beautiful in its own way. My favorite of all: an exquisite *Mary Magdalen* by Lucas Cranach. My second favorite: a bronze plaque of singing angels made after designs by Donatello for a church in Padua. And this is only a cursory glance at what the room has to offer.

Then there's the dining room with its hand-painted eighteenth-century Chinese wallpaper filled with birds and flowers and found near Turin, plus 24 side- and 4 armchairs, also eighteenth century, and lacquered scarlet with gilt-and-silver chinoiserie decorations. They were made in England for a Spanish duke. Not to mention Mrs. Rosen's bedroom with its colossal seventeenth-century wooden bed, carved and gilded and probably designed for Pope Urban VIII. Finally, there's the New Wing, with its early-sixteenth-century Valle d'Aosta Room and Jacobean Bedroom, both brought from the Rosen's New York home.

When you're through inside the house, clear your mind and your (by now) sated senses by taking a refreshing stroll through the grounds and gardens. They have been done to perfection and offer such pleasant surprises as Cedar Walk, with seventeenth-century stone sculptures and, above the festival area, eighteenth-century wrought-iron, gilded gates that are exquisitely detailed.

John Jay Homestead State Historic Site,   Katonah. Open: Memorial Day–Labor Day, Wednesday–Saturday 10–5, Sunday 1–5. Admission: Free. Phone: 914-232-5651 for hours open during rest of year.

You pass this on your way to Caramoor, and it looks interesting. It's not. The home of John Jay, our first Chief Justice of the Supreme Court, it descended in his family through four generations and offers some basically mediocre period furnishings and early American portraits, plus a rather bizarre ballroom added in this century. Unless you are a John Jay fanatic or a distant relative of the family, this is something you can afford to miss.

Some Shops and Galleries   Far more interesting is **Yellow Monkey Village** on Route 35 in Cross River. Without any question, this assemblage of shops in reproduction eighteenth-century buildings will keep you wandering happily about for at least an hour. Be sure to bring your checkbook.

The shop I like best is **The Yellow Monkey Antiques** (phone: 914-763-5848), specializing in English furniture, but it also features wonderful brass and copper utensils. Then there's **Consider the Cook** (phone: 914-763-8844) with everything for the kitchen and pretty Portuguese and Italian pottery. From there you can walk over to **The Cheshire Tree** (phone: 914-763-5732), a flower store, and then go into **Nardin Fine Arts** (phone: 914-763-8451), a handsome art gallery that is a bit overpriced, and **Rosemary** (phone: 914-763-3971), which sells antique American quilts and other decorative items. There's also a confectioners' and gift shop, **Sweet Expectations**, and a tiny lunch room.

While I'm mentioning shops I should also tell you about **Bedford Green Antiques** (phone: 914-234-9273) on the green, naturally enough, in Bedford, which has a large selection of good English and American furniture and decorative pieces. It's a must for your foray into this area.

Finally, in nearby Katonah, can be found **The Katonah Gallery**, 28 Bedford Road (Route 117). Open: Tuesday-Friday, 2–5; Saturday 10–5; Sunday, 1–5. Closed: Monday. Admission: Free. Phone: 914-232-9555.

Founded in 1953, this nonprofit educational institution in an attractive setting presents lively, extremely interesting exhibitions that range from the works of contemporary artists (Kenneth Noland and Ellsworth Kelly, for example) to such diverse topics as "Luminism in American Art," "Northwest Coast Indian Art," "Indians of the Lower Hudson Valley," and "The Face of Egypt." Well worth a visit.

The Hammond Museum and the Oriental Stroll Gardens, Deveau Road, North Salem. Museum open all year, Wednesday–Sunday 11–5. Admission: $2; senior citizens, $1.50; children, $1. Gardens open: May–October, Wednesday–Sunday 11–5. Admission: same as for museum. Phone: 914-669-5033.

The Lower Hudson has several out-of-the-ordinary museums,

but surely this is one of the most charming and a must for garden lovers.

The museum is placed in a setting with a view extending to the Berkshires and Bear Mountain. It was founded in 1957 by Natalie Hays Hammond in memory of her parents and offers both special exhibits and samplings from its permanent collection. How to describe the latter . . . I guess it's a little bit of this (theater memorabilia) and, a little bit of that (some excellent Asian works of art), but the sum of its parts affords an interestingly eclectic viewing experience of one person's highly individual tastes.

What makes it so very special, though, are the Oriental Stroll Gardens, which are divided into such delightful sections as The Waterfall Garden, The Azalea Garden, The Fruit Garden and The Autumn and Zen Gardens. Each is more lovely than the last and there's a mimeographed sheet available written by Miss Hammond that describes what you are seeing. She sets forth its purpose and meanings far better than I: "The translation or adaptation of the Stroll Garden, which originated in Japan and reached its perfection in the Edo Period [1615–1867], should be in terms of tranquility, providing a world apart, as well as a world within. Its calming flowing pattern offers no surprise but special points of interest symbolic of outer and inner windows from which to view the broader landscape or review one's thoughts." Miss Hammond's creation achieves all of that and more.

The museum has one other pleasing element, a restaurant called "Beneath the Bough," that offers excellent food at moderate prices. Best of all, it's set in a shaded flagstone courtyard with a fountain surrounded by geraniums. I would suggest that you lunch here before or after enjoying the museum and gardens. And don't bypass the gift shop, either. It, too, contains a wide variety of pleasant selections. Taken all in all, this is certainly worth a detour.

Sleepy Hollow Restorations

(Tarrytown: A Historical Feast)

GENERAL INFORMATION

How to Get There   The three restorations (each discussed in full below) are all relatively close together: Sunnyside is 1 mile south of the Tappan Zee Bridge on Route 9; Philipsburg Manor is 2 miles north of the bridge on 9; and, for Van Cortlandt Manor, continue north on 9 to the Croton Point Avenue exit, then go one block east to South Riverside Avenue, turn right and, about a half-mile farther on, you will see the entrance on your left.

Hours and Admission Prices   All three buildings are open daily, 10–5, except on January 1, Thanksgiving and Christmas day. Single-visit ticket: Adults, $4; senior citizens and children (6–14), $2.50. Two-visit ticket: Adults, $7; senior citizens and children, $4.50. Three-visit ticket: Adults, $10; senior citizens and children, $6.50.

Year-round special events take place at all three, and you can call in advance for information. Phone: 914-631-8200. All three also have gift shops with a wide selection to choose from, and each offers picnic facilities.

A word of advice: Don't be as ambitious as I was the first time I went and try to see all three on the same day—it can be exhausting. Remember, a three-visit ticket is good for 6 months. You can also get a free calendar of events by writing: Sleepy Hollow Restorations, 150 White Plains Road, Tarrytown, New York 10591, or phone the number listed above.

Sleepy Hollow Restorations, chartered by the State of New York as an educational institution, was put together by John D. Rockefeller, Jr. The project began in 1937 when what is now Philipsburg Manor was to be torn down and replaced by a housing development. Rockefeller stepped in and purchased the house in 1940. Then, in 1945, a collateral descendant of Washington Irving decided to sell Sunnyside. Again Mr. Rockefeller came to the rescue, buying not only the house but many of the original furnishings as well. Finally, in 1953, Van Cortlandt

Manor became available and it, too, was added to the Restorations project and opened to the public in 1959 after the staff of Colonial Williamsburg had restored it.

Today the overall collection includes about 6,000 fine and decorative pieces as well as paintings, drawings, prints, textiles and such from the seventeenth, eighteenth and nineteenth centuries, all offering an unparalleled glimpse of life in the Hudson Valley over a period of 300 years. It is a remarkable project that has been perfectly accomplished.

Sunnyside (Tarrytown)

The approach is much the same as Henry James described it years ago, "a deep, long lane, winding, embanked, overarched, such an old-world lane as one scarce ever meets in America. . . ." It sets the mood for your arrival at this fanciful, endearing confection of a house.

I sometimes think that if I could have my choice of any house on the Hudson, this might well be it. Irving himself described it as "a little, old fashioned stone mansion all made up of gabled ends, and as full of angles and corners as an old cocked hat." It is all of that; if a house could be called "good-humored," it would perfectly describe Sunnyside.

Washington Irving (1783–1859), America's first great writer and still one of our best-loved if only for his short stories based on life in the Valley such as "The Legend of Sleepy Hollow" and "Rip Van Winkle," bought this estate on the banks of the Hudson in 1835. At that time the house was a simple farmhouse built in the seventeenth century when the land was still part of Philipsburg Manor. (In the eighteenth century it was owned by a branch of the Van Tassel family that Irving would immortalize in "The Legend of Sleepy Hollow.") After Irving purchased it he immediately began remodeling to create his own romantic vision of a house with the help of George Harvey, an artist and neighbor whose own home Irving much admired. When finished, it looked almost exactly like what you see today, with those wonderful weather vanes that Irving had taken from old houses in New York City and Albany, Dutch-stepped gables and a wisteria vine over the front door. As for the whimsical, pagoda-like part off to the right, Irving added that in 1847.

Sunnyside still brings out the child in us, like a well-loved picture suddenly rediscovered in an old book of fairy tales.

The interior is completely without pretension, with small, rather modestly furnished rooms made for good conversation and convivial friends. The most interesting to me is the library with its well-worn, rich leather volumes, a red-curtained alcove with a divan where Irving could catch forty winks, and the wonderful, massive desk, a gift to Irving from his publisher, G. P. Putnam.

The dining room, to the left of the entrance hall, is particularly inviting, especially at Christmas when the table is set and decorated with sprays of holly, nuts, fruits and candy, while a large red bow encircles it.

In planning your visit, be sure to leave some time for strolling about the grounds. You'll enjoy the pond Irving created and called "Little Mediterranean"—it is now sailed by swans—and certainly should not miss some of those wooded paths that open up onto views of the river, here at its widest point and looking very awesome indeed.

When you do leave, it's worthwhile to continue south for a

few minutes to Irvington to see the **Presbyterian Church** to
your right on North Broadway. It was built in 1869 by James
Renwick, Jr. (1818–1895), whose most famous building is St.
Patrick's Cathedral in New York City but who also designed the
Renwick Gallery and the first building of the Smithsonian Institute, both in Washington, as well as Grace Protestant Episcopal
Church in New York. The Romanesque Presbyterian Church
here in Irvington, with its exotic cupola and rough-finished
stone work, has the added attraction of windows designed by
Louis Comfort Tiffany, a one-time resident of Irvington. (For an
appointment, phone: 914-591-8124.) Just to the south is the
Gothic **St. Barnabas' Episcopal Church** (1853–63), in charming contrast to its more elaborate neighbor.

Philipsburg Manor (Upper Mills, North Tarrytown)

There's not a child in the world who wouldn't enjoy a visit here
if only to see the grist mill. The miller will let children help him
operate it and it's a lot of fun for them to watch the huge,
clackety-clack water wheel he releases to grind his corn. For
adults it's an informative trip back to the early part of the
eighteenth century to see how a working estate of that time
operated.

Frederick Philipse (1626–1702)—his Dutch name was Vre-
dryck Flypsen—was born in Friesland, Holland, the son of a
slater, and immigrated to New York (then New Amsterdam) at
the age of 21. Between 1662 and 1693, by then a very rich man,
he created his estate, called the Manor of Philipsburg and consisting of 90,000 acres. Philipse had his primary residence in
Yonkers (see page 188) but, in the 1680's, constructed this manor
house, which became the headquarters of the first industrial
complex in the Thirteen Colonies. His son, Adolph, turned the
mill into so successful an operation that its flour and meal was
even shipped overseas, but everything collapsed when Frederick's great-grandson, Frederick III, remained loyal to the British during the Revolution and fled to London. The estate was
confiscated, and the family name disappeared forever from
American history.

Before you visit the mill and stone manor house there is an
excellent 15-minute orientation film you should see. Then your

Looking across the Pocantico to the mill and Philipsburg Manor House, one of the first "industrial complexes" in the country. The Philipse family sided with the British in the Revolution and thereby lost everything.

guide takes you across a wooden bridge over the Pocantico River to view the buildings. The house itself is small—it was, after all, used more as a place of business than as an actual dwelling—and some of the rooms served several purposes. In Adolph Philipse's bedroom, for example, the bed could be folded against the wall when not in use. There also are two kitchens, a foreroom and a parlor, all furnished with superb examples of Dutch, New England and New York pieces.

The mill itself, though, is everyone's favorite, for it is in working order, and the costumed miller is only too happy to demonstrate how the whole thing operates.

When you leave, be sure to visit the **Old Dutch Reformed Church,** built by Frederick Philipse in the 1690's and lying just north of the manor. Its bell-shaped gambrel roof, old when Washington Irving wrote about it, makes it instantly identifiable as Dutch Colonial. Irving is among the famous Americans buried in the graveyard. If you wish to see the inside of the church, though, call 914-631-1123 for tour times. I've found that the building is usually locked tighter than a drum whenever I've visited.

Van Cortlandt Manor (Croton-on-Hudson)

Of all the buildings in the Sleepy Hollow Restorations project this nearly 300-year-old house is not only one of the most authentic but also lays claim to being the loveliest in the group. And perhaps because it is a little off the beaten track, I find that the tours here are generally smaller and more relaxed.

The first Van Cortlandt to come to this country was Oloff (1600–1684), who arrived in 1638. He ended up a highly successful New York businessman and a leading citizen of the city, eventually rising to deputy mayor in 1667. His name is now

Tarrytown's Old Dutch Reformed Church was built in the 1690's. Its graveyard is the final resting place of Washington Irving.

perpetuated in New York City's Van Cortlandt Park (see page 189), part of his original estate that eventually encompassed 86,000 acres. As for this manor, it is Oloff's great-grandson Pierre (1721–1814) who is most associated with it. Pierre lived here as a country gentleman from 1749 onward after marrying Joanna Livingston from another famous Hudson River family (see page 51), and she, according to legend, designed the beautiful "Long Walk" that leads from the house to the tavern.

When the Revolution came, Pierre—unlike Frederick Philipse—sided with the patriots and became the first lieutenant governor of the state in 1777, serving in that position for 18 years. The house descended through the family until 1945, when it was sold. A short time later, Mr. Rockefeller bought it. Much of what you see here in the way of furnishings and other articles belonged to the Van Cortlandts.

This wonderful-looking stone and white-clapboard house has a striking double staircase leading to a pillared veranda on the second floor through which guests would enter, the service rooms being on the first floor. Inside, the rooms have been restored to show the changing taste of the family from the seventeenth into the nineteenth centuries; the parlor, for instance, has Queen Anne, Chippendale and Federal furnishings as well as two handsome portraits circa 1725 and a French mantel clock dating from much later. They go well together, creating a feeling of continuity, of an actual family living here over a great span of time. But my favorite room is the dining room with its mid-eighteenth-century mantelpiece, its shelf supporting Chelsea figurines, and the rare Delft biblical tiles around the fireplace opening. There also is an excellent portrait of Ann Stevenson Van Cortlandt attributed to Ezra Ames (see page 38), painted about 1815, as well as a splendid Federal sideboard.

The downstairs is much more informal, the old parlor and kitchen filled with simpler furnishings and, naturally, more utilitarian objects. If you're lucky, one of the employees may be cooking at the brick hearth and offer you a sample of her fare.

From the house you take the brick-paved "Long Walk" to the Ferry House. This 750-foot-long walk is bordered by perfectly maintained flower beds and there are also orchard and vegetable gardens nearby to reinforce the nicely eighteenth-century bucolic feeling. Both the Ferry House, once an inn, and the

The old Ferry House and kitchen on Van Cortlandt Manor furnish much insight into what eighteenth-century inns were like. The brick "Long Walk" in the foreground leads to the manor house and is bordered by well-kept flower beds.

nearby kitchen were for the use of travelers who crossed the Croton River here to continue on up the old Albany Post Road, the remains of which still exist at the end of the property.

The bar room is terrific, with a stunning collection of pewter, good-looking Windsor chairs and tables. The common room is a bit more elegant and was more exclusive when it was in use, but give me the bar room any day. Upstairs are two dormitory-styled bedrooms for men and women. All in all, an interesting peek at an eighteenth-century inn—but I wonder if it ever looked this inviting and fresh and clean when it was in actual use.

Another Fine House Nearby

Lyndhurst Although not part of the Sleepy Hollow Restorations, Lyndhurst should nevertheless not be missed. It is located about one-half mile south of the Tappan Zee Bridge on Route 9 (a half-mile north of Sunnyside). Open: April to October, Tuesday–Sunday 10–5. It also is open weekends in November and December. Admission: Adults, $4; senior citizens, $3, and children 6–16, $2. Phone: 914-631-0046.

Of all the houses that line the Hudson in a stately progression that demonstrates almost every architectural style, Lyndhurst is the best in the way it complements and enhances the natural splendor of its setting. Put it down on any other spot in the world and it might jar, but here it is absolutely right and, says William H. Pierson, Jr., author of *American Buildings and Their Architects,* "when completed in 1866, [Lyndhurst] was the most profoundly intelligent and provocative house to be built in this country since Thomas Jefferson's Monticello."

The mansion was designed by Alexander Jackson Davis (1803–1892), perhaps the greatest residential architect working in the Gothic Revival style that this country ever produced. Gothic Revival took its inspiration from the Gothic style of the Middle Ages and was the complete antithesis of cool, rational classicism. In its earliest phases, Gothic Revival was all emotion and picturesque eccentricity, and so when Davis was asked to build a great house atop a hill, his imagination was especially fired by the special light and unspoiled magnificence of the Hudson River Valley. His long association with Thomas Cole and other romantic painters of the Hudson River School also stood him in good stead.

Davis erected Lyndhurst, the perfect Hudson River Gothic house, in two phases. The first began in 1838 and was planned for General William Paulding, a former mayor of New York City, and his son, Philip. The second, which roughly doubled the size of the building and created what we see today, was begun by Davis in 1865 for its new owner, George Merritt, a successful merchant and inventor who wanted his house to reflect his wealth—and not in any modest way. The last family to occupy the mansion was that of Jay Gould (1836–1892), robber baron par excellence, who happily bilked the Erie Railroad of millions and then proceeded to come very close to cornering the gold market, thereby causing the panic that is still referred to as Black Friday (September 24, 1869). Since Gould also controlled Western Union and the *New York World* and held vast interests in the western railroads, he could well afford Lyndhurst when he bought it in 1880. (His daughter Anna, Duchess of Talleyrand-Périgord, gave the estate to the National Trust for Historic Preservation in 1964.)

The house, set high above the Hudson with wonderful views to the north and south, has a breathtaking exterior, a fairy-tale palace of turrets and towers, mysterious windows in wonderfully changing shapes and sizes, a superb veranda . . . all seemingly jumbled together in a restless gray mass of Sing Sing marble with no immediately recognizable architectural plan. But look closer and walk around it: you'll soon see that it exudes an inherent logic, power and intelligence that fits it exactly into its setting. The house doesn't look "built," it looks as if it *grew,* its outlines and proportions splendidly matching the Valley it adorns. And the more you look at it from different angles and positions, the more wonderful it becomes.

My favorite place is the veranda, which manages to be a part of both the interior and the exterior of the house. You feel here as if you're moving within a wonderful limbo that contains the best of both the man-made and the natural worlds—protection from the elements in a welcoming space, yet all the joys of the outdoors. It moves, somehow—is it because of the marvelous architectural treatment of the ceiling?—and yet it appears extraordinarily peaceful and inviting. Hours could be spent here, at perfect ease, in this strangely contrasting space that somehow achieves a perfect equilibrium.

The interior, architecturally speaking, fulfills the promise of the outside. Still, for me, it's a vast disappointment; heavy chairs (some designed by Davis himself), ugly statuary, mediocre paintings. It is a study in moneyed nineteenth-century gloom.

Before you leave, though, be sure to walk about the grounds. There are 67 acres in all, dotted with wonderful, ancient specimen trees, particularly copper beeches and cut-leaf Japanese maples. Visit the romantically decaying greenhouse, which seems large enough to hold half the houses in the Valley. Built by Jay Gould in 1881 after the original structure on the site was destroyed by fire, it remains an astounding sight even in its present decayed condition. The main building is slightly more than 376 feet long and 36 feet wide, and there are two smaller wings as well. The design echoes that of the house, although most of the neo-Gothic detail is long gone. The frame is wrought

Lyndhurst is set on 67 acres of land. Not far from the house are the remains of the enormous greenhouse, of which this wing is a part. It was once world-famous for its orchid collection.

iron, one of the earliest uses of it for this kind of construction, and served as a prototype for later conservatories throughout the country.

In its day Lyndhurst was particularly famous for its collection of orchids and palms; in fact, Jay Gould's daughter, Helen, established the orchid collection at the New York Botanical Garden by giving them 230 specimen plants in 1900 from her holdings at Lyndhurst. (Originally the greenhouse here had 14 plant rooms).

In a way it's sad to see all this ruined splendor, but much that is still very beautiful remains. There are also plans afoot for more reconstruction and preservation, and already, off to the side, is a carefully maintained rose garden. I find it both pleasant and nostalgic to wander here.

One final note: In the summer, every Saturday evening from early July usually through mid-August, there are concerts on the lawn given by the Lyndhurst Festival Orchestra, and many people come early to enjoy a picnic in this perfect setting. It costs about $7 to sit in the tent, $5 on the lawn. For further information call 914-631-7766.

NEW YORK CITY AND VICINITY

Some Things to See

The Cloisters,   Fort Tryon Park, Manhattan. (Just off River-side Drive.) Open: Tuesday–Saturday, 10–4:45; Sunday and holidays, 1–4:45; Sunday from May–September, 12–4:45. Closed: Monday. Admission: Donation. Phone: 212-923-3700.

I include this, one of New York's great glories and a personal favorite because, from its terraces and many of its windows, you can see views of the River that are essentially unchanged from the time Hudson first sailed up it. This building, more than any other in the city, fits brilliantly into its river landscape setting and would be totally different in feeling (and the poorer, overall) had it been placed anywhere else.

The Cloisters is a branch of the Metropolitan Museum of Art and has a collection of medieval art that ranks among the finest in the world. The building opened in 1938, and most of its contents were given by John D. Rockefeller, Jr. It incorporates within its walls a twelfth-century chapter house and Spanish apse, sections of cloisters from five medieval monasteries and a Romanesque chapel.

I don't have the space to detail all its wonders, but it would be impossible not to at least mention the Unicorn Tapestries Room with its incredible series, "The Hunt of the Unicorn." Probably woven around 1500 in Brussels, with their endlessly beautiful and complex colors and scenes, almost every inch of the surfaces are covered with flowers and plants, animals and people, all depicted in astounding detail. You could gaze at these magnificent tapestries for hours without penetrating one tenth of their visual feast.

The Hudson River Museum,   511 Warburton Avenue, Yonkers. Open: Wednesday, Friday, Saturday, 10–5:30; Thursday, 10–9; Sunday, 12–5:30. Summer weekends: 12–7:30. Admission: Contribution. Phone: 914-963-4550.

This museum bills itself as "a place of comparison and contrast where stimulating interpretations of American culture interweave art, history and science." Well, yes, it is just that. There's a Victorian house (the 1876 John Bond Trevor Mansion) filled with Victoriana in 3 restored rooms with some selections from the permanent collection on the second floor that, every time I've visited, have been related to the Hudson River Valley.

There's also a modern building containing an attractive gift shop, a planetarium, and a hall of science on the ground level, while downstairs is a large exhibition space. For me, this is where the action is. The shows here are mounted in a highly intelligent manner with excellent descriptive captions. For instance, I remember with great pleasure an exhibit of more than 100 works, primarily drawings and sketches, by Frederic Church and borrowed from a variety of sources. Rarely seen, most of them, they provided a special insight into the character and talents of one of our great artists. Next to it was an exhibit devoted to contemporary American landscape artists that was chosen with equal care and taste. But, then, this museum is always a joy to visit and is usually full of surprises. I find it enormously stimulating.

The Museum of Cartoon Art,   Comly Avenue, Rye Brook. Open: Tuesday–Friday, 10–4; Sunday, 1–5. Admission: Adults, $1.50; students, $1; senior citizens and children under 12, 75¢. Phone: 914-939-0234.

The world's first museum dedicated to cartooning opened its doors in 1974 under the leadership of Mort "Beetle Bailey" Walker.

It is housed in a building known as Ward's Castle (1876), reputed to be the first house in the United States completely built of reinforced concrete. So much for trivia. The edifice is now on the National Register of Historic Places and has a wonderful tower with crenellations like misplaced teeth, plus Tuscan columns and Renaissance quoins. It looks, appropriately enough, like something out of a cartoon. I like it a lot and cannot think of a better home for this museum.

Inside you will be amused by the world's largest and finest collection of original cartoon drawings, magazine sketches and editorial cartoons. Everybody is here; Rube Goldberg rubs elbows with Blondie and Maggie & Jiggs while Superman is unable to impress *The New Yorker*'s blasé Eustace Tilley. Even the carpeting involves such figures as Barney Google and Flash Gordon and, above the stairway, a stained-glass skylight apotheosizes (if that's the proper word here) Prince Valiant and Donald Duck, among others.

No question about it, it's fun to visit and an ideal place to take children. You will leave with a good sensation in your heart and feeling—what else?—a little zany.

Neuberger Museum, State University of New York at Purchase. Open: Tuesday–Friday, 10–4; Saturday and Sunday, 1–5. Closed: December 24–January 2. Admission: Donation. Phone: 914-253-5133.

Philip Johnson designed this spacious museum that dates from 1974. The collections of more than 5,000 works of art is something to behold and owes a great deal to the generosity of Roy R. Neuberger, who made his pile in money management and has had a long-time love affair with American art of the present century. Neuberger wanted his collection to go to a teaching institution and chose SUNY Purchase.

Milton Avery, Mr. Neuberger's favorite painter, is represented by 20 canvases. But there are so many other artists as well that just to list some of the names in the collection should give you a hint of its breadth: Lyonel Feininger, Edward Hopper, Georgia O'Keeffe, Arthur Dove, Frank Stella, Jackson Pollock, Ben Shahn, Jack Levine, Mark Rothko, Larry Rivers, Josef Albers . . . you get the idea. There are even two paintings by Thomas Cole as well as works by Alfred Bierstadt and Maurice Prendergast, but the overwhelming majority of paintings are modern.

My own favorite work is *Threnody* (1973) by Cleve Gray. Gray was born in New York City in 1918 and commissioned by the museum to paint this series of enormous panels. The room that they fill is vast—100 feet by 60 feet by 22 feet high—and Gray chose to fill it with 14 abstract, glowing figures in burningly brilliant colors against a luminous black background. The room itself is in semi-darkness with individual lights concentrated on the figures, shifting male-female forms whose torsos bend and sway in an extraordinary dance of death and life. I think it is one of the great pieces of American art created in the 1970's and, without any question, well worth a special trip to see. Unfortunately, the museum does not keep it on permanent display. Therefore, I'd call in advance. If it's not on view, ask when it will be. Then go as soon as possible. No one with even the slightest interest in contemporary art can afford to miss this monumental and deeply moving masterpiece.

In summer, during July and August, the SUNY campus plays host to *Pepsico Summerfare,* a highly original performing arts festival that can range from jazz and dance to children's opera and theater to cabaret and steel-band concerts. For information, write: Pepsico Summerfare, Performing Arts Center, M.P.O. Box 140, Purchase, New York 10577. Or phone: 914-253-5900.

Philipse Manor Hall,   Warburton Avenue and Dock Street, Yonkers. Open: End of May to October, Wednesday–Saturday 12–5, Sunday 1–5. Admission: Free. Phone: 914-965-4027 for hours during remainder of the year.

One of the best examples of Georgian architecture in New York State, this was formerly the mansion-home of the Philipse family, whose stone house and grist mill on the Pocantico is one of the more popular sites of the Sleepy Hollow Restorations project (see page 177).

The last member of the Philipse family to live here was Frederick III, who backed the wrong horse in the Revolution and wound up an exile in England, impoverished and bitter, while his huge estate, about one third of today's Westchester County, was confiscated by the state and then sold at auction. Before the war, though, he had extended and rebuilt the house and planted extensive formal gardens, now long gone, in imitation of the English aristocracy he so admired.

Today the manor hall is basically empty of furnishings and its interest lies mainly in its architectural detailing, in particular the rococo ceiling in the East Parlor, one of the most handsome and elaborate of such ceilings in the country. There is also a collection of paintings of noted Americans, some copies, some rather good, focusing on American presidents. Of them all, the best is an introspective self-portrait by Eastman Johnson (1824–1906).

Van Cortlandt Mansion,   Van Cortlandt Park. (Near Broadway and 246th Street.) Open: Tuesday–Saturday, 10–4:45; Sunday, 12–4:45. Closed: Monday. Admission: Adults, $1.50; children under 12, free. Phone: 212-744-3572.

Although not as beautiful or as magnificently restored as Van Cortlandt Manor (see page 179), this house, built in 1748, belonged to another branch of the same family and has a very definite charm of its own.

The 9-room mansion is more English than Dutch in feel (but do note the wonderful heads above the windows; typically Dutch) and is built of rubble stone with brick trim around the windows. Inside, much of the collection you see belonged to the family.

Some highlights: The East Parlor, with its handsome Georgian mantel and Massachusetts block-front secretary. In this same room you'll note an adequate portrait of Augustus Van Cortlandt by John Wesley Jarvis (1781–1840), an artist less famed for his paintings than for his sense of humor and for what were then euphemistically termed his "mysterious marriages."

In the West Parlor can be found a pair of portraits (Frances White and her husband Archibald Bruce) by John Vanderlyn (see page 84) and a handsome Hudson Valley Dutch *Kas,* or chest, while the Dining Room contains a portrait of John Jacob Astor, a relative by marriage, by Gilbert Stuart (1755–1828) as well as my favorite things in the whole house: two huge teakwood vultures on either side of the fireplace given to the family by the future English king, William IV, and a British admiral in thanks for the Van Cortlandts' hospitality.

The upstairs also has its moments, in particular the Dutch Room (a seventeenth-century bedroom) and the Washington Room, where—yes—he really did sleep. Best of all, though, at least when I've been there, you're allowed to wander about as you please, without a guide.

Wave Hill,   675 West 252nd Street in the Bronx. Open: October–March, daily 10–4:30; April–September, daily 10–5:30. Closed January 1 and Christmas day. Admission: Free on weekdays; $2 on Saturday and Sunday (senior citizens $1). Phone: 212-549-2055.

What a pleasant spot this is for the first-time visitor. Here is the only Hudson River estate open to the public within the boundaries of New York City, and it's very special. Arturo Toscanini lived here, as did Samuel Clemens and Theodore Roosevelt. All of them loved it, and once you've been there you'll know why.

The grounds sit high above the Hudson and offer a sweeping panorama of the Palisades across the river, the George Washington Bridge and, further south, the city skyscrapers that seem in startling contrast to the pastoral landscape that surrounds you.

Wave Hill was built in 1834 by William Lewis Morris, a New York lawyer. In 1866, William Henry Appleton, the publisher, bought it to use as a summer house. But its real period of glory came when George W. Perkins, a partner in J. P. Morgan & Company, purchased it in 1893 and, over a period of almost 20 years, assembled other neighboring properties until he had himself an estate of 80 acres. While he lived at Wave Hill, Perkins built 8 greenhouses and planted many varieties of exotic trees, using, as his chief gardener, a former royal landscape artist from Vienna. Not one to do things in a small way, Perkins also secured his "vista" as well: he purchased, across the Hudson, that part of the Palisades facing his estate to protect his view and was also instrumental in helping to form Palisades Park in 1912. Perkins died in 1920. In 1960, his descendants donated 28 acres of the estate, its two houses and the magnificent gardens to New York City as a public cultural institution.

The landscaping you see today was begun in 1967, and now there are more than 300 species and varieties of trees and shrubs alone. The greenhouse, part of which is open to the public, has tropical and succulent plants, cacti, and an ever-changing display of flora. But the grounds themselves, full of pleasures and surprises, provide the major interest, with their huge trees, elms and maples, shading the lawns; their herb and old-fashioned flower gardens, and, perhaps best of all, a wild garden that leads up to a pretty summerhouse from which the views are superb . . . flowers everywhere! Below the houses, on a 10-acre plot, a forest project is under way to recreate a native Bronx woodland.

In Wave Hill House there's a small gift shop and the public rooms are devoted to special exhibits and concerts. In summer the grounds display sculpture and are often used for outdoor theater and concerts.

Three River Journeys

The Day Line, Pier 81, west end of West 41st Street, New York City. Cruises: End of May to mid-September. No sailings Monday, Tuesday and Friday. Admission: Weekdays—Adults, $12; senior citizens, $10; children under 12, $6. Saturday, Sunday and holidays—Adults $15; senior citizens, $10; children under 12, $7.50. Phone for information: 212-279-5151.

As with everything else in this world, there's good news and bad news about this full-day trip on the Hudson.

First the good news. Without any question this is the most complete boat trip on the river. You leave New York City at 9:30 A.M., and the first "port of call" is Bear Mountain State Park, where those who wish may disembark and be picked up on the return journey. Then through the Highlands, with another stopover at West Point, and on up to Poughkeepsie where the boat turns around, arriving back in New York at 6:30 P.M. You get a great deal for your money, obviously, and see some of the most beautiful sections of the river.

Now the bad news. Over the weekend and oftentimes even during the week—at least to Bear Mountain, where many people thankfully do get off—this can be a jam-packed excursion and *very* noisy. I strongly urge you to take the trip during the week if at all possible (and even then . . .). In addition, the boat is a relatively modest one in terms of creature comforts and offers very boring food, so bring along a picnic and, if you can, your own chairs, although you can rent them as well as tables on the boat.

Aside from all this, though, I would still suggest that if you have any affection for the Hudson you take the Day Line—once, anyway. The scenery, throat-catching in its beauty and infinite variety, is worth any minor aggravations.

World Yacht Line, Pier 62, west end of West 23rd Street. Year-round schedule. *Dinner Cruises: 7–10 Luncheon and Sun-*

day Brunch Cruises: Check times. *Late Night Cruises:* 12–3 A.M.
Phone for information and prices: 212-929-7090. Credit cards
accepted. Parking available.

The "fleet" of this company now consists of 2 boats, furnished
and decorated with both elegance and comfort in mind. Without
any question, this is the most luxurious way to cruise around
Manhattan and would be an ideal method to show the city off
to a newly arrived tourist. The food is so-so, the service more
friendly than efficient, but neither is terribly important considering the real charm and comfort of these boats as well as the
extremely romantic setting. Definitely worth a try by even the
most jaded New Yorker.

The Circle Line, Pier 83, west end of West 42nd Street.
Cruises: April to mid-November. Operates 7 days a week. Ad-
mission: Adults, $12; children under 12, $5. Twilight cruises:
June–August. Phone for information: 212-563-3200.

By the spring of 1984, more than 34 million people had taken
this 3-hour, 35-mile-long cruise around Manhattan. I had not
been among them. More the fool me, for as I had been told ad
nauseam by everyone who had taken it, this little trip is a must.
Now I think I may make it an annual event.

Before the trip, though, some tips. First, everyone rushes for
seats on the open top deck. Don't. I did, but soon realized that,
no matter how much the crew complains, everyone is going to
stand, taking thousands of pictures, and it's soon like the subway at rush hour. So I went downstairs where there were
fewer people and just as good a view for all of the east side of
Manhattan after the Brooklyn Bridge. (Stand or sit on the
port—left—side facing forward, if possible.) I would suggest remaining outside for the first part of the trip past the Statue of
Liberty and up the East River to Brooklyn Bridge and then
going inside, returning on deck only for the part going back
down the Hudson. Another good place is on the bow, where
people tend to come and go, and you're more likely to get a
good spot. Second, the commentators are wonderful—I've
heard three of them now—and do try to listen to some of their
spiels.

At first I was a little disappointed after the boat began its run;
New York City, New Jersey and the Hudson do not blend into

a ravishing sight at this point, but then, as you move out into
the Upper Bay and see Ellis Island and the Statue of Liberty
and finally swing around to look at that world-famous view of
Lower Manhattan in the sunlight, it's hard not to get a lump
in your throat. On up to the Brooklyn Bridge (1883), designed
by John Augustus Roebling (1806–1869)—he died of tetanus
after his foot was crushed by a wooden piling during the early
days of the bridge's construction—and completed by his son,
Washington (1837–1926). For me it's the most special bridge in
the world and the only good justification I know of to see the
East River. Then up the East Side; basically dull if you know
New York, but with one or two nice moments—the UN building, for instance. Things pick up, though, as you go through the
Harlem River Ship Canal at Spuyten Duyvil and they race
when you return back out onto the River, this "great romantic
stream," as Henry James said, "such as could throw not a little
of its glamour . . . over the city at its mouth." "The sordid city,"
he added elsewhere, "has the honour, after all, of sitting there
at the Beautiful Gate." He had his priorities exactly right: The
River graces the city, not the other way around.

The first and most obvious glory is the Palisades Ridge, that
unique landmark that extends for 50 miles and soars as high as
827 feet above the river. Here, from the river, it is a series of
awe-inspiring columns, marching north over the horizon and
south to the bay, an ultra-glamorous setting from which the
Hudson will make its dramatic exit. Then there's the George
Washington Bridge (1931), a silvery, elegant 4,760-foot strand of
steel that was designed by Othmar Hermann Ammann (1879–
1965), a civil engineer also responsible for the Verrazano-Nar-
rows Bridge (1964). For me the brilliance of the George
Washington Bridge, aside from its basic beauty (Cass Gilbert
served as consulting architect), is how well it suits the river; it
does not bestride it, like some vulgar conqueror, nor does it
hesitate tentatively at the great leap it must make. Rather it
looks like a companion, a natural addition to the scene and one
of the few man-made ones that neither uses, in the commercial
sense, nor abuses the magnificence of its setting.

After that it's a series of wonderful impressions as the great
River passes Manhattan (*pace,* Henry James): There's The
Cloisters and Grant's Tomb and Riverside Baptist Church and

Morningside Heights and then the great skyscrapers . . . and
. . . and, a little sadly, the Upper Bay, where the Hudson disappears from sight, still to run its final course to the edge of the
Continental Shelf. There it will end at last, in one more burst
of splendor, as an underseas falls. How I wish I could see
that!

Where to Stay and Eat

Putnam, Orange and Westchester Counties
Area Code: 914

Where to Stay: Three Inns and Two Hotels

The following are listed in order of preference.

Hudson House, 2 Main Street, Cold Spring 10516 (Putnam
County). Phone: 265-9355. Rates: For a single, from $60; for a
double, from about $70. Includes breakfast. Credit cards ac-
cepted. Closed in January.
   The Hudson Valley's choicest place to stay in its most dramatic setting. (For a description of the inn, setting and food, see
page 149.) Reserve well in advance.

The Bird & Bottle Inn, Route 9, Garrison 10524 (Putnam
County). Phone: 424-3000. Closed: First two weeks in January.
Four rooms. Rates: From $155, modified American plan. Credit
cards accepted.
   This old clapboard inn, yellow with black-and-white trim, was
established in 1761 and has just about everything an inn should
have—fireplaces, beamed ceilings, wide plank floors and antiques scattered liberally about, including canopy or four-poster
beds. It's a visual delight. (For the food, see page 201.) Reserve
well in advance.

The Golden Eagle Inn, Garrison's Landing, Garrison 10524
(Putnam County). Phone: 424-3067. Five rooms. Rates: Monday–
Thursday, from $50 for a double; Friday–Sunday, from $60 for

a double. Two rooms share a bath. Price includes continental breakfast. Credit cards accepted.

Another very pretty, small inn, this time an 1848 red-brick Federal building on the banks of the Hudson and offering a grand view of West Point, which is directly opposite. The host and hostess, George and Stephanie Templeton, are gregarious, the rooms spacious and brightly decorated by Stephanie, a former interior designer. By the way, the inn served as the setting for Horace Vandergelder's store in the film *Hello, Dolly!* and a permanent reminder remains in the etched "V" of the glass front-door panels. A friendly, informal place you'll enjoy. Reserve well in advance.

The Tarrytown Hilton, 455 South Broadway, Tarrytown 10591 (Westchester County). Phone: 631-5700. Rates: For a single, from $75; for a double, from $90. Credit cards accepted.

I'm not a great fan of Hilton hotels, but this one is surprisingly attractive and does not look like it came out of a cookie cutter. For instance, good-looking prints line the walls and, in the bar, framed antique quilts add a nice homey touch. The service is professional and friendly, the facilities excellent— heated pools, an exercise room, tennis, saunas, the whole bit. The food is lackluster, but you can't have everything. Reservations are usually not a problem.

Hotel Thayer, West Point 10996 (Orange County). Phone: 446-4731. Rates: For a single, from $35; for a double, from $50. Credit cards accepted.

Government-owned, this hotel has splendid river views from many of its rooms. It's a little too big and rather bureaucratic for my taste, and the food is boring at best, but if all the above inns are booked it's a pleasant enough alternative, and you're right smack in the Highlands. Reserve well in advance.

Where to Eat: Six Favorites

Dozens of restaurants sprinkle the Lower Hudson, but I have only listed those that, for one reason or another, I have truly enjoyed and feel can be recommended, even with some reservations. Unlike the other two regions of the Valley, there are no great restaurants, but you can dine very well all the same, particularly at the six places I have listed below as my favorites. In addition, prices at many of them approximate those found in New York City and, again as in New York, French cuisine predominates. I would also like to register a formal complaint that the wine prices at French restaurants are ridiculously high (again New York's baleful influence) and I now tend to stick to the house wines, thereby saving a measurable percentage of my yearly income.

Buffet de la Gare, Hastings-on-Hudson (Westchester County). Phone: 478-1671. Credit cards accepted.

Don't be misled by the setting, a slightly seedy area of Hastings, or the building, undistinguished and unpretentious—to put it kindly. Inside the tiny interior is charming with pressed-tin walls and ceiling, fresh flowers in abundance, a handsome old oak bar, lace curtains, not to mention Victorian chandeliers and wall fixtures. As for the food, it's excellent. The French menu is smallish, featuring six or seven entrées plus two or three specials, but everything is first rate and the selections avoid the obvious. I would recommend duck in any form they decide to prepare it; it's always done to perfection. And if cassoulet is on the menu, go for it; it's very good. The wine list, for once, is reasonably priced and offers several nice selections. Overall, you will dine very well in this pleasant bistro that could have been transported here directly from France. Moderately expensive. Lunch: Tuesday–Friday, 12–2:30. Dinner: Tuesday–Friday, 6:30–9:30; Saturday, two sittings, 6:30 and 9:15. Reservations essential.

La Crémaillère, Banksville (Westchester County). Phone: 234-9647. Credit cards accepted.

A particularly inviting French country restaurant in an old house with wall murals of peasants in native costume from different provinces, fresh flowers everywhere, soft pink tablecloths, handsome china, dark wood beams and copper and brass pots filled with dried flowers and grasses. The family who run this restaurant also own La Caravelle in New York City and have established a high reputation over the years for first-rate food and service, but now it seems like they're coasting on their reputation. The service is good—but if you're not a regular you can sometimes feel they're pushing just a bit too much to get you through your meal and out the door. The menu is lovely, with a wide selection of entrées, but the special care and attention that go to make a dish memorable is lacking. Still, thanks to the ambience and overall quality, it's a pleasant enough place to dine, although no longer an exceptional restaurant. The wine list, incidentally, is superb, with corresponding prices. Expensive. Lunch: Tuesday–Saturday, 12–3:30; Sunday, 1–8. Closed Monday. Dinner: 6–9:30. Reservations essential.

Mona Trattoria, Route 22, Croton Falls (Westchester County). Phone: 277-4580. Credit cards accepted.

Housed in a wonderful 1864 Victorian white-frame building with a broad veranda, this is my favorite Italian restaurant in the area. The food is delicious—veal scaloppine with truffles and Parmesan cheese and a homemade tortellini al ragù spring to mind as particular favorites—and the selections numerous and thoughtful. The Italian wine list, I might add, is small but well planned and reasonably priced. Even the desserts—one of my prejudices is that Italian restaurants in this country usually have desserts built around brick-hard spumoni—are good. Friendly service and an attractive atmosphere top it all off, and the prices are reasonable. I recommend it highly. Dinner: Wednesday and Thursday, 6–10; Friday and Saturday, 6–11; Sunday, 3–9. Closed Monday and Tuesday. Reservations suggested.

Plumbush, Route 9D, Cold Spring (Putnam County). Phone: 265-3904. Credit cards accepted. Moderately expensive. Lunch: 12–2:30 daily except Tuesday. Dinner: Monday, Wednesday–Friday, 5:30–9:30; Saturday, 5:30–10:30; Sunday, 2:30–8. Closed Tuesday. Reservations necessary. See page 150.

René Chardain, South Salem (Westchester County). Phone: 533-6200. Credit cards accepted.

The Chardains used to own one of the best restaurants in Vermont, The Four Columns, and it was there that I first enjoyed their marvelous food. Now they've moved south, to this much more elegant setting in a turn-of-the-century stone-and-frame house with particularly striking fireplaces and the same first-rate food. One of my old favorites from the Vermont days, an Indonesian chicken curry, still graces the menu and is still as perfectly prepared. But there are new additions, and I particularly remember one special: a lovely piece of salmon, brushed with mustard, topped with Mornay sauce and then popped under the broiler. The restaurant also offers an excellent selection of cheeses. A very pleasant experience. Expensive. Dinner only: Tuesday–Saturday, 6–9. Closed Sunday and Monday. Reservations suggested.

The Box Tree, Purdys (Westchester County). Phone: 277-3677. No credit cards accepted.

One of the best restaurants in the Lower Hudson and very different in feel from its namesake in New York City. This one is in an old white frame house, unpretentious on the outside, and you enter through a small, attractive bar. The dining rooms are lovely, with comfortable tapestried chairs and antique tables, the walls decorated with paintings and handsome sconces. You are immediately put in the mood for an excellent dinner, and you get one. The cuisine is on the nouvelle side in the best sense of the word: willing to experiment without going off the deep end. One spring night I had a grilled salmon with Béarnaise sauce that was, quite simply, the best I've ever had—and the added hint of lime complemented it to perfection. I should also point out that the wine list is thoughtfully chosen and the prices won't ruin your dinner. Dining here is expensive but not outrageous, and the food is worth every nickel. Dinner only: Monday–Friday, 6:30–9:30; Saturday, two seatings, 6:30 and 9:-30; Sunday, 6–9.

Other Restaurants Worth Noting

Auberge Argenteuil, 42 Healy Avenue, Hartsdale (Westchester County). Phone: 948-0597. Credit cards accepted.

This restaurant, like so many, is in a converted house with dining rooms scattered about in enough profusion to make it surprisingly large. Decorated in a vaguely French Empire style, it's pleasant enough, with efficient service. The food is well prepared, and they have game in season that can prove special.

It's moderately expensive, but they give reasonably good value for the price. Lunch: 12–3 daily except Sunday. Dinner: Monday–Thursday, 6–9:30; Friday and Saturday, 6–11; Sunday, 1–8:30. Reservations required.

Auberge Maxime, Route 116, North Salem (Westchester County). Phone: 669-5450. Credit cards accepted.

Homely on the outside, but within the small dining room is both attractive and comfortable. The restaurant specializes in a wide variety of duck dishes—including pressed duck, which must be ordered in advance—and those that I have sampled are very good. A prix-fixe restaurant, this one averages about $40 per person for a full dinner, and as with all prix-fixe menus, I rather resent it. I don't need all that food and wish I could simply order what I want instead of feeling I'm being stuffed for the kill. In any case, it is good but the price remains excessive. Lunch: 12–2, closed Wednesday and Saturday; Sunday, 1–3. Dinner: Monday–Friday, 6–9; Saturday, two sittings, 6:30 and 9:15; Sunday, 3–9. Closed January. Reservations necessary.

Beneath the Bough, The Hammond Museum, Deveau Road, North Salem (Westchester County). Phone: 669-5033. Credit cards accepted. Lunch: Wednesday–Saturday, 12–1:30; Sunday, 12–3. Dinner: Wednesday–Sunday, 6–8. Reservations unnecessary. See page 173.

Gasho, Route 32, Central Valley (Orange County). Phone: 928-2387. Credit cards accepted.

There are brochures everywhere for this restaurant, so I put off going for a long time thinking it would be mobbed with people and probably not very good. I was right on the first point, wrong on the second; the food is not only good, it's also very reasonably priced. Another surprise is that the restaurant itself is so very attractive. Located in a farmhouse that was moved here from Japan, then reconstructed, it's surrounded by flowers, a Japanese garden, water wheels and a teahouse. The tables are communal, a grill in the center of each, and the food is cooked right there before you in one of those displays of Japanese dexterity in chopping, mincing and dicing that always makes me afraid one of the chef's fingers may wind up in my rice. Lunch: Monday–Saturday, 12–3. Dinner: Monday–Friday, 5:30–11; Saturday, 5–11; Sunday, 12–10. Reservations unnecessary.

Hudson House,   2 Main Street, Cold Spring (Putnam County). Phone: 265-9355. Credit cards accepted. Moderately priced. Lunch: Monday–Friday, 12–2:30; Saturday, 12–3; Sunday brunch, 12–2:30. Dinner: Monday–Thursday, 6–9; Friday and Saturday, 6–10; Sunday, 5–9. Closed in January. Reservations necessary. See page 150.

Le Château,   Route 35, junction Route 123, South Salem (Westchester County). Phone: 533-6631. Credit cards accepted.

Set on 32 acres with pleasant views, this brick-and-stone house was built by J. P. Morgan in 1907 as a gift for the rector of St. George's Episcopal Church in New York City. The interior is rich with paneling and fine craftsmanship. If only I could say as much for the food. The service is adequate but lacks that extra touch of the true professional. The menu is standard as is much of the cooking—beef bordelaise, chicken of the day, calf's liver and so forth—but the specials can be quite good; one night, for instance, I had venison that was perfectly cooked and served in a creamy rich brown sauce. But the wild rice that accompanied it was overdone, the vegetables watery and unbuttered, the bread stale. You win one and you lose one—or three —but the restaurant is expensive and the food should be more carefully prepared and presented. Lunch: Tuesday–Friday, 12–2. Dinner: Tuesday–Saturday, 6–10; Sunday, 2–8:30. Reservations suggested.

Maxime's,   Old Tomahawk Lane, Granite Springs (Westchester County). Phone: 248-7200. Credit cards accepted.

Maxime Ribera, chef-owner, used to be the proprietor of the Auberge Maxime (see page 199), then sold it and went south. He's back now and is running this establishment. The restaurant is comfortable, reasonably attractive, and the service is excellent. I would suggest you ask for the room with the fireplace when reserving as the dining area by the bar is atmospherically chilly. The food is good. Nice touches: hot hors d'oeuvres served with your drinks; delicious, home-made sorbets as a palate cleanser before the entrée; first-class desserts. Expensive. Prix-fixe dinner: About $37. Lunch: 12–3, closed Saturday. Dinner: 6–9, closed Monday. Reservations necessary.

Nino's, Bedford (Westchester County). Phone: 234-9852. Credit cards accepted.

On the outside, all is white-frame, New England picturesque. Inside, and you know you're in an old-fashioned Italian restaurant with bad to worse paintings and (you hope) good food. Well, ignore the décor and your expectations will be fulfilled. The menu is more northern than southern Italian—cannelloni, for example, has a delicious, subtly light sauce—and all the pastas are homemade. The service is efficient, the food excellent, the prices moderate. My only complaint is that the desserts are not very good. Lunch: Monday–Saturday, 12–2:30, closed Tuesday. Dinner: From 6, closed Tuesday. Reservations necessary.

The Bird & Bottle Inn, Route 9, Garrison (Putnam County). Phone: 424-3000. Credit cards accepted.

The dining room, long and warmly lit, its walls hung with handsome prints, is appealing and offers a near-perfect setting for a romantic dinner. And the food is quite good—their black bean and pea soups and roast pheasant, especially—but I don't list the place among my favorites for two reasons: the kitchen lacks consistency these days and the food can be overly rich. It certainly is worth a try, though, and if they're up to the mark that night you'll enjoy a superior dinner at a reasonable price. Lunch: Monday–Saturday, 12–2:30 à la carte; Sunday brunch, 12–2:30, prix-fixe at about $13. Dinner: Monday–Friday, 6–9:30; Saturday, two seatings, 6 and 9; Sunday, 3–7. Prix-fixe dinner at about $30. Reservations necessary.

INDEX

About the Author

TIM MULLIGAN is an (almost) lifelong New Yorker. He was educated at Phillips Academy, Andover, Yale University and the University of Paris. He has been both an editor and writer for several national magazines including *Travel & Leisure, Holiday, New York, Good Housekeeping* and *Cosmopolitan.* He is also the author of *Virginia: A History and Guide.*